PRAISE FOR ALISON CARDY CAREER COACHING WORK

"Before working with Alison my mind was in a million directions and my ego was trained to tell me 'no' and steer me in the exact opposite direction of where I wanted to go! I needed an outsider's perspective. Since our work together I'm clear on where I'd like to go. Alison is an expert at what she does and an inspiration."

— K.K., Travel Coordinator

"I began the process skeptical of the whole idea of life/career coaching and cynical about the possibility that it might help me in any way. By the halfway point of the first session, both feelings had melted away. Alison manages to walk the tightrope of empathizing like a close friend while providing an insightful diagnosis of the problem like the objective professional that she is. I would recommend her services to anyone who is floundering or searching for guidance in life or career."

— J.K., Lawyer

"Before working with Alison I felt lost and trapped. I was convinced that I would never be able to leave my job and find something more fulfilling. Alison helped me realize that I am a good employee, and that better options do exist. She helped me make my first cold networking connection, an action of which I was previously terrified. As a result of working with Alison I am more confident that I will be able to find a more fulfilling job."

— R.Z., Technical Project Manager

"I had a wonderful experience working with Alison and truly feel in a better place after our time together. After our last session I felt like I had a clear idea of where I needed to head and what to do. This is a feeling I had not had since before graduate school. I am refreshed and refocused."

— A.G., Director of Business Partnerships

"I truly wasn't quite sure what to expect when I initially signed up for the program, but working with Alison completely exceeded my expectations. Her calm demeanor and "life will be okay" perspective was great match for me. I also greatly appreciated her commitment to staying current on the job market and being so knowledgeable about different resources. Overall, this experience was incredibly positive and beneficial!"

— R.M., Education and Literacy Advocate

"I was not sure of what to do and whether my feelings with regard to my job were healthy. Working with Alison helped me understand who I am and, specifically, what is most important to me. I am now okay with knowing that I have a creative side, even if I don't make a living at it."

— N.R., Mechanical Engineer

"Before working with Alison I felt lost in terms of my career. I didn't have a clear idea as to why I wasn't happy with my job, and I wanted to discover a more suitable career path for myself. Now things are going great. I love my new employer and place of work. I like what I am doing, and not only do I see potential for growth, but so do they! I will be recommending Alison in the future—she's great!"

— A.K., Executive Assistant

"Alison listens, draws up a plan, discusses options with you, keeps you on track, acknowledges your effort and comes up with amazing solutions that makes you go 'what???'. And it works. Even after my coaching with Alison finished, I can hear her talking whenever I'm at a loss for what to do. Whenever I slip back into my comfort zone she appears in my head and reminds me of the outcome of inaction."

— S.H., Cost Analyst

"I enjoyed Alison's demeanor and support, but mostly I was amazed at how many sessions were incredibly productive and helpful. With Alison as my coach I really made some life changes! Alison, thank you so much for everything and for all of your nonjudgmental help. I loved your approach, and I appreciated your flexibility."

— J.M., Graduate Career Advisor

"Before working with you I was lost. I knew I needed to move, but I didn't know where to go. You kept me in check and made me focus on what action I should take. You were also kind and understanding in listening to my situation."

— E.H., Marine Biologist

"I was feeling rather directionless in my career and unsure how to begin to make a change. Alison acts as a great sounding board to listen to my varied thoughts and was able to succinctly point out where my mindset was holding me back. From our work, I'm feeling more confident that I am on the right track."

— T.H., Art Museum Giving and Campaign Manager

"I was vacillating between trying to pursue my former career and trying something else entirely. Alison really helped me understand, without directly telling me, what the answer was to my question. Then she reinforced my decision with feedback."

— M.T., Senior Project Manager

"Before working with you I was confused and doubting myself and just all over the place in terms of what direction I was going. You inspired me, gave me clarity, and helped me align with what I want."

— K.A., Actress and Film Producer

"I was struggling to understand my frustrations at work, and how that was impacting my personal life. Alison helped me assess my problem from a totally different perspective, which really helped me to move towards a solution. THANK YOU THANK YOU THANK YOU. Our sessions have really opened my eyes to how I struggled, and gave me real strategies to help me improve things."

— M.O., Foreign Service Officer

"Working with Alison was especially helpful because it gave me specifics–making the list of what I wanted and researching companies that would be a good fit. Some of it had been there all along (and over time to my surprise), and I just needed to see the light."

— S.W., Accountant

"Alison is an extremely genuine, kind-hearted person. She is smart, thoughtful, creative, and has excellent values. I thought she listened and received everything I had to say during our work together."

— J.B., Labor Organizer

"As a result of working with you I am no longer thinking myself in circles, and I have taken real world steps towards a life I want to build. The anxiety that guided my decisions (or lack thereof) is no longer there. I had a wonderful experience with you!"

— S.R., New Graduate

"Before working with Alison I was stuck in a cycle of inaction, or ineffective action. Working with Alison was helpful because she is EXTREMELY patient and able to adjust her plan for me as she saw fit. She was a positive support while guiding me through exercises that pushed me outside of my comfort zone."

— G.T., Artist and Community Programs Manager

"Before working with Alison, I was extremely frustrated with my lack of progress in searching for my career path and was feeling defeated. I had for the most part given up on the possibility of finding a new career that would excite me. In our work together, Alison was extremely patient and was able to help guide me to a place where I felt re-energized and focused, with a clear strategy for next steps. It was a pleasure to work with her."

— A.O., Program Officer

"Thanks again for all of your support. I could not have gotten this far without you. I mean that sincerely."

— B.Z., Contract Negotiator

"Most of all, thank you for all of your guidance these past six or so months! It's been a long journey and you've helped me sharpen my focus on things. I'm glad you turned up in my Google search! Keep changing lives! :)"

— E.A., Communications Specialist

"I wanted to thank you again for the time you spent with me, and let you know that based on our conversation I've taken a few action steps like we discussed! Thank you, thank you, THANK YOU for being a part of my journey!"

— E.B, Nurse and Hospital Manager

"Thanks for the great help, I have been very happy and impressed by what we have accomplished so far. You are a great coach!!"

— E.H., Reading Intervention Specialist

"I got the job!! :) THANKS! Just think- a couple of months ago we were talking and who knew what was coming! I am incredibly thankful for this opportunity."

— S.C., Sales Associate

"I did a session with you maybe a year ago about finding what I really want to do with my life. I wanted to share with you that I have my dream job now. Exactly what I wanted. I went from a frustrated retail worker to leading a fun team of people creating really great content for our fans. Our talk helped me get focused. I appreciate what you do!"

— K.O., Social Media Manager

"I appreciate you helping to get me to this point by reflecting back to me what my inner voice is asking for, and providing tools to overcome fears. Thanks again for your effective + gentle guidance in the right direction."

— J.S., Education Human Resources Department

"You have been the best 'medicine' for my daughter. You have given her confidence and encouragement, and great advice. I am so grateful on many levels."

— K.M., Interior Designer

"So far my work is going well, and I've been really happy! I also really love the team and their work/life balance and friendliness -- it seems like people really love working there and also have other things going on in their lives. On the whole, it feels really gratifying to work in a place where a lot of different parts of myself get to be present (and valued!) at once. So, at the moment, I feel open to the future and great. I feel more brave and excited about piecing together the job and life pieces that make sense for me. Thank you again for your help in this transitional moment, and I do appreciate your checking in!"

— L.F., Writer and Non-Profit Marketer

"Thanks so much!!! It's so helpful to have someone supportive even though I know I have made a series of mistakes. It helps to see the way forward despite that and in a warm supportive way. I appreciate your assistance in helping me see the carrot and not just the stick. Your calls come in as a ray of hope to me."

— P.V., Physical Therapist

"Thank you again for taking time to speak with me today. It really helped to discuss my situation with someone with experience and new ideas. I really appreciate it, and, already, I'm feeling better."

— C.W., Market Researcher

"Thank you for everything--without you, I'm not sure that I'd have been able to make the career-change I needed. I hope you're doing well! The job is going wonderfully! I love my team of coworkers, I enjoy (my work), and I've learned (a ton). There is A LOT I can take advantage of under one roof to help me develop professionally, and I already have the network set up!"

— S.R., College Health Department

"I was browsing through old emails this morning, and I came across our conversations from two years ago. Reading them over, it really hit me how helpful you were when I was going through a difficult time and how grateful I am for the career-guidance you gave me. I'm in the second year of my job, and I absolutely love it. So many of the things that you helped me realize I needed in a job—collaboration, freedom, growth, teamwork—are exactly what I love about what I do now."

— P.F., Teacher

PRAISE FOR ALISON CARDY'S KEYNOTES AND WORKSHOPS

"Alison was a dream to work with. She is not only flexible, but also delivers a terrific, well-organized presentation. She commands a room and captured and held our audience's attention. She was able to fill over an hour with her material while speaking and incorporating interactive group break-out sessions. We had nothing but positive feedback and rave reviews. We had many great takeaways from her presentation."

— Martha Naughten, Commercial Real Estate Women DC

"I just wanted to let you know that Alison Cardy was an awesome speaker! She was articulate and informative. I especially appreciated that she was willing to stay after so we could ask her specific questions about our own situations. I would definitely recommend bringing her back for a future event."

— Attendee at Cornell Alumni Event

"Alison walked in the room with a great attitude and immediately won over the trainees with her presentation. She was extremely knowledgeable and helped trainees work through some of the thoughts that were holding them back from progressing. She left them with useful tools that will undoubtedly help them move forward. We can't wait to have her back!"

— Deniece Pope, Lead Trainer, Career TEAM DC

"Whether you are unsatisfied with your current career and its trajectory, have hit an inflection point, are looking for a new challenge, or a student looking to start something promising, career coach Alison Cardy will have a solution for you. Her interactive presentation kept the audience engaged and I came away with quite a number of solid new takeaways–even considering the fact that I have already changed careers more than once."

— Mark Bershatsky, DC Net Impact

"Your workshop was amazingly helpful to me because I have been trying to figure out my life after college. I am a worrier and a planner, so I get myself freaked out. Your seminar was incredibly helpful in just reminding myself to take a breath and remember it all doesn't have to be figured out right away. Your session stuck with me in so many ways, and I am so thankful I had to opportunity to hear your speak."

— Attendee at PLEN360 Summit

"Alison's workshop on salary negotiation was fantastic. Not only did she clearly and effectively present salary negotiation basics, but her presentation was also interactive, engaging, and fun! I would recommend her to any group."

— Roya Vasseghi, Co-Chair of the Women's Bar Association of the District of Columbia's Solo & Small Practice Forum

"Alison was a pleasure to work with—she made pulling together a program easy! The insight she provides during her talks are applicable to anyone, no matter the career stage. Her facilitating is top notch, too. She's able to handle the bigger personalities in groups and reel the conversation back on topic if it gets off track. We'd love to have her back again soon!"

— Natalie Neumann, Association for Women in Communications

"Thank you for leading such an engaging, informative session last night. I learned a lot and really enjoyed your presentation style (the two hours just flew by!). I especially appreciated your coaching technique, which can be applied to other areas of life beyond my career. Thanks again!"

— K. Kramer, Association for Women in Communications

"It was a pleasure having you come and speak! I don't think that I have ever seen so many folks wait around after the event to talk with the speaker, which I think is a good indicator of how well you engaged people."

— Dana Kaasik, Graduate Research Assistant, Center for NonProfit Studies at George Mason University

"Alison's salary negotiation talk helped me negotiate a 20% salary increase, signing bonus, and relocation assistance when I was accepting a new job. Most importantly, Alison's workshop gave me the confidence to successfully navigate multiple rounds of negotiation while maintaining a constructive and friendly relationship with my future employers. Her insights and teaching style helped me tremendously, and the information I gained from this workshop will continue to serve me in many other professional and personal situations that require negotiation."

— Salary Workshop Attendee

"Alison worked diligently to develop content, find a venue, and recruit fellow alumni clubs to join Cornell alums in a career planning session. Alison presented worthwhile information to a group of about 60 guests, with a networking session to follow, further adding value to the event. She was communicative and easy to work with and the event was a success for all!"

— Lindsay Shattenstein, Young Alumni, Cornell Club of Washington, D.C.

"You were just perfect!!!! Thanks, Alison, so very much! Our folks are so hungry and appreciative when someone takes the time to be with them. You have given them valuable tools for a lifetime. For that, The HUB is grateful. I would very much like for you to return to our group for another speech in the future."

— HUB Organizers, Tysons Corner, Virginia

"Before attending Alison's salary negotiation workshop, I only had a rough idea of how to ask for a raise. But I had no idea how to present myself in a professional manner for the presentation; she gave us strong examples of how to bring in materials, what words to use, and most importantly what to avoid."

— Salary Workshop Attendee

"I have been on both sides of the negotiation table–but it wasn't until I participated in Alison's workshop that I was able to understand the psychological dynamics of negotiating–from both perspectives. An eye opening experience."

—Salary Workshop Attendee

"Before I attended Alison's Negotiating presentation, I was not confident about handling salary negotiations. Now, I feel like I have the tools to discuss salary requirements during an interview and negotiate a salary that I can be happy with. Thanks for the tools!"

— Salary Workshop Attendee

CAREER GREASE

HOW TO GET UNSTUCK AND PIVOT YOUR CAREER

ALISON CARDY

Career Grease: How to Get Unstuck and Pivot Your Career

ISBN 978-0-6926-5451-4
2016—First Edition
Printed in the United States of America

Cover and Interior Design | Melissa Tenpas —www.MelissaTenpas.com
Interior Design | Lindsay Gomez —www.LindsayGomez.com

DEDICATION

To my readers—
May you have the courage to do the hard things.
May you have compassion for yourself along the way.
May you choose to live a life that's your own.

ACKNOWLEDGEMENTS

For several years the idea of writing a book floated in the back of my mind. Then one day my savvy colleague, Christine Clapp, a speaking coach and owner of Spoken with Authority, told me, "Do it now. Write your outline and get it done." Christine was not only a catalyst for my writing, but also a beyond generous guide throughout the writing and publishing process. I am incredibly grateful for her support.

Lindsay Gomez rocked my world with her diligence, creativity, and organizational products. Her assistance helped me to step into a bigger vision for my business. Lindsay, thank you from the bottom of my heart for paying attention to all the details, keeping me on track, and being a wonderful collaborator. It's been an absolute pleasure to have you on my team.

Mia Tawason, my longtime assistant, supported me for years behind the scenes with a wonderfully positive attitude and excellent follow through, allowing me to focus on working with my clients.

Charlotte Lieberman, my editor, enhanced my writing and clarity with her keen eye and skill with language. Melissa Tenpas guided me through the final stretch of book design and publishing with kindness and insight. Rachael Moser capably supported me with developing, organizing, and executing my book launch and promotion strategy. Members of my community generously participated in my Book Advisory Council. I'm still amazed at how wonderful these folks have been to me.

Thank you for your perceptive feedback on my ideas and for the encouragement you showered me with during the final stretch of this project.

My phenomenal client base has given me the honor of stepping into their lives for a moment in time. You inspire me with your courage, your persistence, and your willingness to do uncomfortable things in pursuit of your goals. I've loved having a front seat view of the positive changes you've made or are working on. (I know that they never come fast enough, but you're doing great!) I'm over here cheering you on and celebrating each and every win you have.

A number of people have been particularly positive and helpful to me over the years. Jenny Shih, Jen Choi, Sarah Yost, Brenda Wille, Becky Barnes, Stephanie Cox, Anne DeMarsay, Ludovica Valentini, Heather Miller Cox, Frederique Irwin, Rebecca Dallek, and Laura Labovich—you've all made a difference to me with your friendship, calls, notes, support, and insights. Thanks!

My mom, Ellen Horner, has been the encouraging voice on the other end of the phone for many evening calls. Thanks for being the first reader of this book, believing in me, listening to all my grand plans, and letting me know that it's OK to have a bad day every now and then.

Lastly, a huge shout out to my husband, Dan Cardy, who has stayed by my side through my own career ups, downs, and loop de loops. You've given me logistical and technical support every step of the way—a beautiful roof over my head, your tech savvy, and time listening to whatever I'm going through. Thank you for all your generosity, patience, and backing. You're my anchor. I'm able to be level headed when supporting others because you keep me so cared for and grounded. I love you lots. Muah!

CAREER GREASE

CONTENTS

CAREER GREASE

FOREWORD

By Laura M. Labovich of TheCareerStrategyGroup.com

Holly strode into our office for her first interview coaching session convinced she was sabotaging herself in her interviews. We spoke at length about this answer and that. I pulled repeatedly from my bag of interview tricks, but she knew every . . . single . . . one.

Holly was deflated. When she spoke of her target job, it was as if she were reading the ingredients on a bag of Oreos. Despite being articulate and talented, and clearly suited for the job to which she was applying, I just could not get excited listening to her.

About 90 minutes into the session, she asked, "So, Laura, what's wrong with my interviewing skills?"

I paused, reluctant to share my findings.

"Holly," I began, "Do you really want this job?"

Hedging, she said, "Yes."

I followed up with, "Why?"

Her eyelids dropped, and she thought briefly before replying, "I'm just ready to leave my company. It's time."

"I get that it's time to leave . . . but is this the type of work you really want to be doing?" I inquired.

"It used to be. But along the way . . . things have changed. I'd really love to do something else. If I'm being honest . . . I don't want to do this anymore."

Holly is not alone—not by a long shot. According to the oft-cited (but never verified) statistic, the average American will change jobs seven times in his career.

And there are also those who stay in a job they hate. They stay because they've been told they must (most often by that little voice in their head, but sometimes by a parent or spouse). They stay because they believe that leaving would be quitting, which would be shameful or wrong.

Or, they stay because changing careers is just something they don't know how to do.

But, Alison Cardy does.

In *Career Grease*, Alison clearly identifies the path from A to Z: the path from old to new, from stuck to empowered. By debunking career myths right and left and sharing a protocol for transitioning to a new path, she enables career changers to move through fear and raise their confidence—all to "get unstuck" and achieve what they most want from their careers. (I especially love the "Categories of Stuckness"—brilliant!)

I have been sending my career change clients to Alison for years because of her natural ability to create structure and clarity around such a confusing, frustrating, vague, and ambiguous process as career change. *Career Grease* is, to me, a career change bible. Carve out a space on your shelf next to *What Color is Your Parachute*. This book is equally helpful (and not nearly as long)!

To your career success,
Laura M. Labovich
TheCareerStrategyGroup.com

INTRODUCTION

Your brain will entertain the idea of making a career change any time your career path is at odds with what you're most wanting in life. You might be bored or unfulfilled with your current work, craving greater financial stability, or yearning for more time to take care of yourself or your family. Whatever the reason, once dissatisfaction enters the picture, your thoughts will naturally move towards solving the problem at hand.

In an effort to figure out what to do next, you've probably attempted one or more of the following actions:

- taking assessments or personality tests;
- looking at graduate programs or job boards;
- talking the situation over with loved ones, friends, or mentors;
- dreaming about an ideal situation; or
- assessing the financial realities of making a change.

At some point in the process of trying to figure out a better career direction, you got stuck. Time has passed. You still don't like where your career is headed, so you're still dissatisfied. But now you're also dealing with the frustration of not making progress. You may be starting to wonder if you will ever move your career to a better place.

If any element of the above description resonated with you, then you're just like my career coaching clients. And with that, I've got good news: you've picked the right book.

Career changes are irregular—and difficult—occurrences for most of us. Very capable, smart, and resourceful people often feel lost and overwhelmed by the process. They don't know what career choice would be a better fit for them, and they are at a loss for how to begin figuring it out.

I've guided hundreds of people through career changes and improvements. As a result, I know the full landscape of the process—including the reasons why you've stalled out and the steps necessary to get you moving again.

While the specifics of each client's career journey differs, the general process I guide my clients through follows an identical framework that allows them to get unstuck and successfully achieve a concrete improvement in their lives.

This book will teach you this process. In the first two chapters, we'll go over the foundational elements you'll need to have in place to get started. In Chapter 3, I'll share a ten-thousand-foot view of the steps involved in making a career change, so you can know exactly what to expect. In Chapters 4–10, I'll break down the most common reasons why people get stuck at a career crossroads, and I'll provide you with instructions for maneuvering through these issues. Chapter 11 will give you a glimpse at the entrepreneurial career path (I know you've thought about it!), and Chapter 12 will tie everything together and encourage you to keep your momentum going strong.

Throughout the book, I'll tell you stories of the struggles and successes of real clients who have put in the effort and bettered their careers. (Of course, names and identifying details have been changed to protect confidentiality.) I'll also share my favorite career coaching concepts and exercises to help you avoid unproductive missteps, and I'll debunk the most common and precarious career myths I see people buying into. I know how frustrating it can be to feel stuck, so I've put my best strategies and frameworks into this book to help you get moving.

One last thing before we get started. I know books can sit unopened on night stands. Strategies can go into the nebulous mental cloud of "I'll get to that someday." Our best intentions can be forgotten. So to further assist you, I created a complimentary companion to this book that will help you keep on track with handling your career crossroads situation. If you're committed to finally solving your career conundrum, you can give yourself an added layer of support and accountability by signing up for the Step-by-Step Career Change E-Course at www.cardycareercoaching.com/bookgift. It's a totally free resource, my gift to you.

If you sign up, you'll receive an email from me with a reminder of a bite-sized action step to take each week, along with encouragement to help you stay motivated as you maneuver your career to a better place.

Go to www.cardycareercoaching.com/bookgift to receive the Step-by-Step Career Change E-Course.

I'm looking forward to supporting you in making a positive change. I get a kick out of being helpful, and I hope this book makes a huge difference in your life. I often tell my clients, "This is a solvable problem!" Let's get to work on solving it ... together!

Chapter 1

ASSESSING YOUR READINESS FOR POSITIVE CHANGE

People experiencing career-related dissatisfaction often reach a critical point at which they're ready to shift from thought to action. In this chapter, I'll tell the story of my first conversation with a new client to give you a sense of what that "readiness" looks like. I'll have you assess your own readiness and identify the type of career shift you're craving.

Amy, a married mother of three, had been working as a corporate mediator for a firm in Seattle, Washington for eight years. When she and her husband initially moved to Seattle for her husband's job, Amy found it difficult to gain a foothold with her career in the new city. She floated around for over a year and eventually took her current mediation job out of desperation to have any job at all.

Now, eight years later, Amy is burnt out. She doesn't enjoy her work and generally feels stuck—though she still has a glimmer of hope that she could find a better-fitting career path. She's worked with career coaches before and has taken every personality assessment available, including the Meyers

Briggs (several times). But she has not been able to make the switch to a new career. She felt skeptical about reaching out for help again. However, she knew that what she had been doing on her own hadn't been working.

During our initial conversation I asked Amy to tell me a bit more about what had been happening. She said that she was disengaged with her work. She felt completely out of sync, unfulfilled, and perpetually drained by her all-encompassing job. Since she had three small children, her "free" time was often spent on family matters; she had little time (and energy) left in her to put towards figuring out her career.

I asked Amy to consult her imagination and connect with what she wished her next career move would look like—not the specifics, but just the general attributes she was ideally looking to get from a new career.

"Oh, I want something completely different," Amy told me with enthusiasm. "I want more flexibility. I want work that energizes me and is more creative. I want to engage with my work rather than feeling like I am continually pushing myself just to get through it."

"So if where you are is an ill-fitting position, and where you want to be is in a job that matches up more with who you are and what you care about, what is currently getting in your way of going from where you are now to where you want to be?" I questioned.

"Well, it's a couple of things. My husband is supportive, but he has his own things going on and doesn't really know how to help me with this transition. We both value the financial stability my current job provides for our family, which makes it hard to consider a change," Amy explained, citing very valid reasons for her uncertainty.

"Also," she continued, "I talk myself out of pretty much any idea I come up with. When I do see a possibility, I wind up focusing on all the reasons why it would never work."

"Gotcha. What you're describing is typical for the clients I work with. Many of them have been stuck for a year or many years—and they're really good at talking themselves out of potential career paths, just as you described. So you came to the right place. I specialize in helping people who are stuck at a career crossroads. We're going to approach things a bit differently than the other career coaches you've worked with so that you can actually gain traction and make progress," I explained.

"That sounds great. How does it work?" Amy asked.

I wanted to provide Amy reassurance and concrete details, so I dug into my archive of client stories to give her a sense of how I work.

"Let me tell you a quick story of a former client of mine, who was in a very similar situation and made it to the other side," I began. "Vanessa was in her forties. She had a law degree, small children, and had been feeling stuck with her career for over ten years. Sound familiar?" I joked.

"Very much so," Amy replied.

"For years, Vanessa had been trying to figure out how to improve her career. It was a heavy weight that sat perpetually on her shoulders. While she thought about her career all the time and often entertained the idea of switching profession-al gears, she hadn't been able to actually *do* anything about it. That's where I came in. Vanessa and I worked together to identify what she actually wanted most from her pro-fessional life. From there, we cleared up the psychological obstacles that were coming up for her, and I supported her in taking productive actions to move her career forward. It took some work and time, but Vanessa eventually landed a part-time internship in the exact field and organization she wanted. That internship turned into a full-time position one month later."

"Wow," Amy said.

"Plus, her new job provided her with the flexibility she was looking for in order to be able to be with her kids. I always try to keep in touch with my clients, and Vanessa still loves her job, is learning a lot, and feels so relieved to have brought this essential aspect of her identity more into the foreground of her life."

"Wow," Amy said again, now with a hint of hope in her voice. "That's really good to hear."

"Yup, this is what I do. I help get people unstuck and on a more productive path with their careers. I know all the places and reasons people tend to get tripped up. Over the years I've developed a toolbox of exercises that are really good at getting people back on track," I explained to Amy.

It's common for people to feel confused about their career direction. The reason for this confusion is simple yet profound. Careers are not incidental choices. In fact, they have the potential to satisfy us—or disappoint us—in three huge areas of our lives: 1) our fulfillment, 2) our financial health, and 3) our personal time and well-being. It's easy to get a bit spun around when trying to balance each of those weighty elements.

After describing this concept to Amy, I reassured her, "I can help straighten things out for you. Together we can figure out what you want, what's getting in the way, and how to clear those obstacles. We'll develop a plan to get you to your goals."

I knew I could help Amy. But before making any claims, I always like to assess how committed my clients are to improving their lives. I wanted to check in with Amy about how willing she was to put in the effort required to make a change in her life.

"On a scale of 1–10, how ready are you to get your career sorted out?" I inquired.

"I'm a 10," Amy said without hesitation. "This has been going on for too long."

I knew Amy and I would make headway together, and I felt so glad she had reached out. Of course, I let her know that we wouldn't necessarily be able to get her into a new job immediately. But I was confident I would be able to give her a big ol' shove in the right direction.

Amy was more than ready to make a change in her life. She was tired of feeling so stuck, and she wanted help. I got the sense that Amy would be a motivated and active participant in the coaching process. She wanted to understand what she was missing and was eager to learn how to move through the obstacles that were holding her back so that she could increase her level of happiness with her work.

CORE CONCEPTS

DESIRE AND WILLINGNESS TO MAKE A CHANGE

No one can change your life but you—and that goes for any aspect of life, no matter the magnitude of the shift you are seeking. In order to be successful in the career change process (and remember: it is a process!), there needs to be a strong sense of motivation and a willingness to do, and feel, things that are new and uncomfortable.

THREE CAREER DESIRES + SIX CAREER STRATEGIES

Based on my own journey and my years of working with clients, I've isolated what I call the three Career Desires: 1) fulfillment, 2) financial health, and 3) personal time and well-being. While we're all hoping to live happy, wealthy, and healthy lives, it's rare to have careers that provide for us at a high level in all three areas at the same time. Due to real world constraints, most of us choose (consciously or unconsciously) a career strategy that provides for us more heavily in one or two of the Career Desire areas that are most important to us.

When the strategy you've been employing no longer matches up with your current priorities, you'll inevitably feel dissatisfied. This sense of dissatisfaction may feel unbearably acute, or it may feel constant and muted. But at some point, you are going to begin considering a change.

For example, you might have been working a high paying, stressful job in order to meet your Career Desire of financial health. That worked well for you until the day you received a physical health scare that had you reassess your priorities. You're now finding yourself thinking about a potential job that would allow you to take better care of your physical well-being, and your old strategy of emphasizing financial security at all costs no longer aligns with your new set of priorities.

See if you can identify which strategy you've been using from the list of the Six Career Strategies presented below. Notice that each strategy comes with an inherent set of risks and rewards. Most of us will change strategies during our lives to keep up with shifting priorities, so also look to identify which strategy currently appeals to you.

I've listed the three strategies that relate to a wholeheart-ed focus on just one of the Career Desires first, followed by the three strategies that illustrate a combination of two of the Career Desires.

FINANCIAL HEALTH FOCUS

The financial health focus implies that you focus your career decisions solely around financial rewards. You may be merely focusing on establishing financial security, or you may be someone who typically finds themselves on the hamster wheel of achievement, constantly looking to reach that next level of financial success (or other external accolades).

Risk Factors: You may find yourself so focused on climbing the career ladder that your vision for other areas of your life becomes obscured. Your health may suffer from strenuous demands. You may get too good at postponing fulfillment

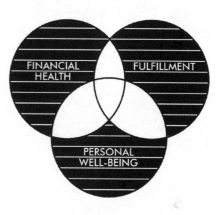

and never give yourself the opportunity to do what you truly want. You may miss out on engagement with your work while you are in saving mode. You may make up for your dissatisfaction with work by spending much of what you earn.

Rewards: You'll undoubtedly feel proud of your accomplishments. You may not have to worry about your financial stability for most of your life, because you'll have thoughtfully saved for retirement and rainy days. You may feel more freedom and have greater financial resources to pursue a second act later in life.

FULFILLMENT FOCUS

A pure fulfillment focus implies going after work that you love at all costs.

Risk Factors: Your investment in your work may not pay off financially. Your retirement savings will be hurt if you are not earning much in the early stages of your career. You may struggle with handling unexpected bills or health issues.

Rewards: You'll have an enjoyable day-to-day life, spending time doing work that you care about. You'll be developing and growing in your areas of strength. Plus, as a result of this personal fulfillment, you'll (hopefully) be living a healthy life.

PERSONAL WELL-BEING FOCUS

This option involves directing your full attention on your family or personal well-being. You could be a stay-at-home parent, someone who steps out of the workforce to care for a loved one, or a person who takes a sabbatical.

Risk Factors: Stepping out of the workforce may make re-entry more challenging. You'll likely face a temporarily diminished earning potential. There's also the possibility that you're using your interest in your family as a way of postponing a decision about what to do with your career. As a result, you may feel lost as to what to do with your career later in life (if you decide you want one).

Rewards: You'll feel meaning in working with the people you care most about—your family. You may be more integrated with your community, which meets your social needs. You'll experience moments of love and have fulfilling life experiences and memories.

FINANCIAL AND PERSONAL WELL-BEING INTERSECTION

The intersection of finances and personal well-being implies attending to your financial health and being present for your family or your individual pursuits. You may work part time and be with your family part time during the week. Or you might work with the motivation of caring for your family or paying for your hobbies.

Risk Factors: You may find yourself resenting your family at times, particularly if you are sacrificing a lot in your day-to-day career pursuits for their benefit. Your dedication to work and family, or personal pursuits, may not go as far as your potential might indicate, simply due to your split attention.

Rewards: You find meaning in caring for your family financially and spending time with them. You keep a foot in the profession-al world, which makes it easier to develop your career or return to work after kids are older. You may get to be present for many important moments with your loved ones. You may create awesome memories outside of work.

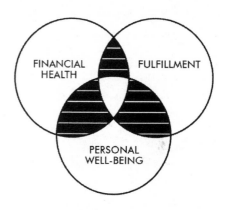

PERSONAL WELL-BEING AND PASSION INTERSECTION

This intersection involves doing what you love and caring for your family. A common arrangement is a small business or hobby profession coupled with being the main caretaker for a family.

Risk Factors: You may feel overwhelmed as a result of your attempt to keep multiple balls in the air. The early years of running a business are often lean, and the failure rate of small businesses is high. Your financial success will likely be compromised, particularly in the initial years of your work. You may feel behind with your career accomplishments.

Rewards: You'll learn new skills and feel proud of developing a source of income for your family. You'll have flexibility to participate in family life and work. You'll be more primed to re-enter the workforce as a result of your continued efforts to develop professionally.

FULFILLMENT AND FINANCIAL INTERSECTION

The intersection of fulfillment and financial health involves honoring your interests and keeping an eye on your financial bottom line. You likely work a day job while investing personal time into other meaningful pursuits.

Risk Factors: You may not be as successful in terms of career milestones because you are not looking for growth; you're only focused on paying the bills. You will likely wish you were spending more time engaged in the fulfilling pursuits you do on the side.

Rewards: You are able to take care of yourself financially and have gathered a cushion of wealth to support you in the future. At the same time, you're also honoring yourself and your interests in other areas of your life. You may be setting yourself up to transition to what you most want to be doing down the road.

We each have individual tolerances for how much meaning we're looking for from our careers, how much money we aspire to earn, and how much free time we want to have to spend on self-care, with our families, or on our hobbies. We also have ranges in each of these three areas that are intolerable to us based on our values and priorities. It is these tolerances that guide our career decisions and which career strategy we choose to employ.

LOOKOUT!

You may be wondering about the intersection of all three Career Desires, and that's a perfectly healthy impulse. Note that this intersection isn't readily available—which makes sense, as it's called a career path for a reason. No one is able to fulfill all of their dreams and check the boxes of their priorities without a lot of hard work. Getting to know what we want, and finding a way to make it happen, is a demanding endeavor.

In other words, finding a career that allows all three Career Desires to intersect isn't available right away for many of us. It's not an option for the career-changer who is re-booting their life in a new field and has to start building their reputation over again. Nor is it available for the person working on cultivating their passion who hasn't found financial success yet. It's not available to the stay-at-home mom who has not developed her earning capacity in the workforce or to the person working a high paying, but unfulfilling job. That's not to say these people can't ever get there—it's just not something that happens overnight.

Enjoying your day-to-day, achieving some traditional notion of success (whether that be financial or reputation-oriented), and having your health and familial relationships in order is not something that will fall into your lap. Period. The process of developing a quality of life in which you can tend to these various aspects is a process—and will only happen through consistent effort and attention, compromise and persistence, trial and error, and a fine balance of courage and compassion. This can take years of work to achieve, and not everyone gets there via their career path.

Luckily, we're all capable of living rich lives outside of this top tier intersection. In fact, we can have high life satisfaction while emphasizing only one or two of the Career Desires if the elements we focus on match up with what is most important to us. We can also be satisfied with our lives with ho hum or non-existent careers through non-career related means (like family, healthy habits, and hobbies) when those are the things that mean the most to us.

I'm a fan of supporting my clients in getting into whatever section of the above diagrams that suits them and what they're wanting most. I don't believe that one path is right for everyone or better than another path. It's about what's right for you.

There is only one path that I would not advise—it's one that is not represented on the graphic. That's to accept an ill-fitting career path as the status quo of your life from a position of resignation. I believe everything improves with attention, so I inherently dislike the idea of ignoring your career by drifting along. My advice? Wake up! Each of us only lives once, so it's imperative that we not waste this precious life by checking out. Make the attempt to strategically improve your life and career by aligning with your priorities.

Throughout the course of this book, I'll provide examples of how people identify and move toward the career strategy where they'll most readily thrive. I'll help you to find the best conditions you can at this moment and strategize for improving your career as you go.

Here's a gentle reminder that you'll also need to take action to make progress on your career. For weekly reminders of the most effective action steps you can take to move forward, sign up for Step-By-Step Career Change E-Course at www.cardycareercoaching.com/bookgift. You can think of these resources as the alarm clock that catalyzes your multi-step process of awakening to the life you want to live. The same way an alarm clock doesn't physically wake you up, this book and the related e-course won't change your career for you— so don't let reading be the only step you take. Remember to follow through on the suggested steps!

EXERCISES

CAREER CHANGE READINESS

Let's take a look at your situation. Our goal is to connect you with your desire for change and to increase your awareness of what's going on. Sometimes we're so enmeshed in our own situation that we don't take time to step back and look at what's happening with a new perspective. Answer the following questions as though you were explaining your situation to someone who had never met you before.

What's going on with your career at the moment? What's not working?

_____

_____

_____

_____

_____

_____

_____

How would you like things to be? You don't have to know the specific career—I know that's why you're reading this book! List the general elements you would like to have present in your next career move. What big picture things are you craving?

_____

_____

_____

_____

_____

_____

_____

_____

What obstacles are coming up for you as you try to move from where you are to where you want to be?

_____

_____

_____

_____

_____

On a scale of 1–10, how ready are you to invest time and effort in resolving this issue?

_____

IDENTIFY THE STRATEGY THAT BEST SUITS YOUR PRIORITIES

Which of the Six Career Strategies did you resonate with when you first entered the workforce?

_____

_____

Which of the Six Career Strategies feels like the best fit for where you are in life right now?

_____

_____

_____

COACH'S NOTE

Many of my clients have been dealing with the status quo for a long time. As a result, they doubt they'll ever make a change. I'm here to tell you that it is possible. I've seen transitions occur time after time. I've been delighted by the forward progress my clients are able to make when they're shown the way. I know you can make progress too.

As you begin learning the core concepts, completing the exercises, and taking the recommended actions you will feel a sense of relief. You may notice an increase in engagement, hope, excitement, and enthusiasm. You'll feel clearer, more connected to the "real" you, and more comfortable with yourself and your career. You'll be able to make compromises to help yourself make progress.

That's not to say every step on this journey is going to be easy. Getting somewhere different means doing things differently. It means trying out new behaviors and perspectives. You're going to feel uncomfortable. At times it will feel like you're taking one step forward and two steps back. But I'm sure you're up to the challenge. Remember that change is possible. I'm going to show you a new way of looking at things that is going to make this puzzle so much easier to solve.

Remember—this is a solvable problem.

Did you go to www.cardycareercoaching.com/bookgift to sign up for the Step-By-Step Career Change E-Course to receive an additional level of support and encouragement? Get to it! It will remind you to stay the course and see this positive change all the way through.

CAREER MYTH: YOU CAN FIX A LOVED ONE'S CAREER ISSUE FOR THEM

One of the questions I'm frequently asked when I'm out speaking to a group is this: How do I motivate someone I care about to improve their career?

At the root of this question is a more general urge that we all have from time to time. In essence we're asking, "How do I get someone else to do something that I know would be good for them?"

This impetus can take many forms. Maybe you've wondered how you could help a significant other lose weight. Or you've thought about how you could make a parent happy. Or you're perpetually dropping hints about how much better off a friend would be if they left that un-hip neighborhood.

These instincts are well-intentioned, no doubt.

But they're also super likely to fail for one simple reason.

I bet the person you are trying to motivate to make a change never asked you for your help.

Since they didn't ask for help they either 1) haven't acknowledged that anything is wrong or 2) their attention is on something else at the moment.

There's a moment when an individual decides that it's important to them to make a particular change and begins seeking (asking) for information that would help them in their endeavor. Until that point it's fairly certain that any tip or strategy you might provide them with will be a waste of breath. Unsolicited advice is easy to give and even easier to dismiss.

We all come to things in our own time.

SO WHAT CAN YOU DO TO HELP THAT PERSON THAT YOU CARE ABOUT RIGHT NOW?

1) Love them unconditionally. That means showing up for them with kindness and acceptance. It also means leaving any agenda that you might have for them at the door.

2) Work on your own life. While you may not have any control over when a loved one decides to make some improvement, you do have control over yourself. Put your time and energy into your next area of growth. Be a light and an inspiration for the people that you care about.

Help is best when asked for, and it can only work when the other party is ready to receive help. You wouldn't throw a baseball at someone until they were facing you with their glove ready to receive the ball. Help works in pretty much the same way.

Are you reading this book for you? Are you ready to receive support and guidance? Is now an appropriate time to be digging into this work? If so, let's get to it! The next chapter will help you with one of the most coveted components of career transitions: figuring out what it is you want!

Chapter 2

CONNECTING TO YOUR CORE CAREER THEMES

---

*Uncertainty tends to be one of the greatest
sources of angst for people when it comes to
career changes. Most people find themselves
thinking, "Man, if I just knew what I wanted to
do with my life!" But here's the thing: identifying what you want out of your career is actually
the easy part of this process, particularly when
you have an objective third party to help you put
things into focus. That said, getting to know ourselves—"digging deep"—is a lot like pulling a
vegetable out the ground. Dirt comes up with it!
In this chapter, I illustrate the process of helping
my client, Sergey, unearth his core career themes.
Chapters Four through Ten will teach you some
techniques for cleaning up the psychological dirt
that you will likely unearth in the process.*

Sergey had earned his bachelors in Biology from Emory
University in Atlanta, Georgia with the intention of attending medical school immediately upon graduation. However,

his participation in the demanding schedule of a collegiate athletic program (Sergey was a soccer player) affected his grades in his freshman and sophomore years. Even after leaving the team in the fall of his junior year, Sergey struggled with the abstract nature of his Biology and Chemistry courses. Through hard work and perseverance he raised his GPA and eventually mastered the subjects that initially troubled him.

Sergey took the MCAT and applied to medical school during his senior year of college. After an anxious wait, he received the disappointing news that all of his applications had been rejected. Sergey picked himself up by his boot-straps and resolved to apply again in several months with a stronger application. With this goal in mind, Sergey took a job working as a lab technician at a research lab in Atlanta focusing in genetics. He also began re-studying for the MCAT in the hopes of improving his score.

Five years later, Sergey was still working in the lab, a dead-end job that most people use as a temporary resume builder. He felt gun-shy about attempting the medical school application process all over again and was feeling deeply stuck in a state of limbo—between an unfulfilling job and an increasing sense of hesitancy about whether the medical school track was even right for him.

When Sergey wrote to me, his state of confusion was palpable: "I do not know what I want to do," he stated plainly. "I have begun to sour on the idea of going to medical school, but I also find myself reluctant to give up on this potential career. I have so many ideas in my head about things I think I'd like to do, but I lack the confidence to drop everything I have earned so far to pursue something totally different. I'm afraid I might sour on that too."

Sergey had reached a point where he was ready to get help with the indecisiveness, fear, and lack of confidence he'd been experiencing for so long. He signed up for my Career Direction Clarity + Action Plan program. This is my mid-tier career coaching program, which guides participants through the process of a career change from A-to-Z. It's a great fit for people who know they have several areas to work through beyond identifying their preferred career direction. In Sergey's case, we needed to address the impact of his past decisions, take a look at the role of his social environment, and work together to boost his attitude so that he would begin believing again in his chances for success. This program's longer-term support system made the most sense for his situation.

When I begin working with a client, regardless of the particular issues at hand, I have them complete a series of open-ended questions before our initial session. The questions are thought-provoking and intended to point us in the direction of the client's strengths, interests, and dreams. They are not designed to be a strict aptitude or personality test. In fact, I shy away from those materials because they tend to be reductive, putting people in boxes. I'd rather meet my clients exactly where they are to create a customized assessment. Career paths are highly individualized, and I want to base all my work with a client on a comprehensive understanding of who they are and what they're most wanting.

My goal for my first coaching conversation with Sergey was to identify the core themes that were most important to him and his career. During this initial session with my clients, I play detective and kindly pepper our conversation with questions to get to know them and support them in clarifying their desires. As we talk, I listen for changes in energy and enthusiasm. I make informed connections between the reactions I pick up on. After this, I test out mini- hypotheses throughout the conversation. For example, if I notice that interpersonal relationships are a factor in client's work satisfaction, I may ask "Do you like being out in front of customers or are you more a behind-the-scenes person?" If clients show a history of involvement with non-profit organizations and/or volunteering, I will try and probe their motivations and goals. I may ask something like, "Was your volunteer experience in Africa appealing because of the cause you were supporting, the type of people you were working with, or both?"

I often think of this initial conversation as taking an image seen by an out-of-focus telescope and bringing it into focus. Everything is already there. The client just needs help seeing it clearly. I serve as the outside party that helps put things into perspective.

Here's a snippet of my first coaching conversation with Sergey to illustrate what I mean:

"During today's session, I'm going to ask you a bunch of questions to get a better understanding of who you are and what's important to you in your career. The goal is not to pinpoint exactly what you want to do next, but to identify the components you're most wanting. It's usually a fun conversation because we'll be talking about a lot of things that you like," I said to Sergey to introduce the session's work.

"Ok, sounds good," he replied.

"Let's start with soccer," I began, bringing up a topic that may not seem directly career-related, but was definitely important to Sergey. "As I read through your pre-work responses it was clear that this was a large part of your life. I'd love to hear more about it."

"Well, I started playing soccer when I was young. I'd bounce around and play whatever position the team needed. I liked it because two of my best friends were on the same rec league team. We'd horse around and play soccer with one another most nights after school. We all lived on the same street. Then in high school, soccer was the main thing on my mind. I was really focused on trying to get better. I'd work on my game anytime I wasn't at school or doing homework. I learned a lot of life lessons from soccer—how to work hard, how to be resilient," Sergey recounted.

His last point caught my attention. "What did you like about soccer once you began to really focus on it in high school?" I asked.

"I liked that it was a group of people working together towards a common goal. It was interesting learning the intricacies of the game and being athletic," Sergey told me.

"And in college?" I probed further. I sensed from his pre-work answers that there may have been a shift in his attitudes about soccer.

"Things changed in college," he confirmed. "I didn't enjoy it as much. I was no longer one of the best players, and I wasn't as integral to the team. No scouts were looking at me, and I started questioning all the time I was putting towards something that wouldn't pay off. That's why I decided to quit the team during my junior year to focus more on academics. Right now I don't play, and I do miss it sometimes," Sergey explained.

My line of questioning was deliberately about soccer—but not because I thought Sergey should make a career out of soccer and become a professional athlete. I was curious to understand the way he had interacted with the sport when it was such a big part of his life. After this quick chat, it sounded like his motivation stemmed from striving for excellence, especially with a team focused on a common goal.

"OK, got it. Let's move on. One of the experiences you listed really enjoying as a kid was working on cars. Tell me more about that," I said with a smile.

"That was the other thing I did as a teenager. When I wasn't playing soccer, I was messing around with cars. I really enjoyed learning about the engine and all the different parts. It was cool to see how everything came together to work. My dad brought home an old Volkswagen Bug that didn't work at one point, and I would just go out there and fiddle with it to try to fix it. I'd research the different parts and try to diagnose what wasn't working," Sergey described.

The same way I saw something deeper in Sergey's reflections on soccer, I knew there was something to this hobby too. "Do you like working with your hands?" I asked.

"That's part of it. I think I do a lot better with things that I can see. When I was in school, I struggled with cellular biology. Reading about the concepts didn't do it for me," Sergey explained. "But I remember this one class where they showed a video about all the parts of the cell, which included these 3-D models of how everything worked. That's what made it click for me. So yeah, I think I do better when I can touch and see what I'm working on," he elaborated, sounding relieved at the realization he had made based on my question.

"Interesting. And when you said you researched the mechanics of the VW Bug, did you enjoy that process?"

"Oh, I got really into it. When I'm faced with a concrete problem, I'll read everything I can get my hands on to figure it out. I don't really think about it. I just want to get a full understanding of what's going on so I can apply a solution. That's what I did with my parents' shed too."

"What do you mean?"

"My mom wanted a little room off to the side of my parents' house where she could work in peace. She sells metal jewelry part time, so it was going to be like a little office for her. She told me what she wanted the room to be like, and I talked to her about ventilation requirements—you have to have good airflow when you're working with metals," Sergey recounted with a sense of enthusiasm. "I then spent about two to three months researching and planning every aspect of building the space she wanted—all the dimensions and the materials we'd need, how I'd handle the electric and the ventilation. Some of my mom's ideas weren't feasible, but I liked figuring out what we could do and making her space better. I got really caught up in it."

"It sounds like you were trying to optimize your mom's shed design for her."

"Yeah, I hadn't ever really thought of it like that, but I'm always strategizing, trying to make things better. Even when I started building the shed for her, I'd pay attention to little details to make the space more functional for her. I thought quite a bit about outlet placement, trying to figure out where it would make the most sense. The exhaust fans were another thing I took a lot of time with."

"So what was most engaging for you as you were working on this shed for your mom? Was it the research, the design, or the actual building of the structure?"

"It was everything, really," he admitted. "I liked figuring it out and creating the space. I liked seeing the tangible result. I even liked calibrating the ventilation system. It was sort of tedious, but I knew how important it was, so I rigged a mechanism to track the airflow through the system. I kept a journal to track all the changes I was making to see how they impacted the ventilation. I'm really organized like that and pretty methodical. I stick with something until I figure it out."

Sergey and I talked over a number of other experiences from his life, and we found that a lot of his interests echoed the shed story. After reviewing all my notes, I compiled a list of his core career themes—the things that he'd likely most want to have present in his next job. It was apparent to me that the Career Strategy that would likely be the best fit for Sergey would be the intersection of Financial Health and Fulfillment. He wasn't earning much or enjoying his current job, so improving both elements would be priorities as we moved forward.

"OK, I have a list of your core career themes here. I want you to listen to the themes and imagine that you're working in a job that has all of these elements present. Just pay attention to your reaction. Let's see if we're on the right track," I instructed Sergey.

"Sure."

"You're in a job where you're optimizing the functionality of a physical thing—something that you can see and touch. Your work involves researching, planning, designing, and building. You can see how your work helps other people. You get to utilize your mechanical mind and make things better, probably as part of a high functioning team. Take just a moment and try to bring that to life in your mind's eye. How does it sound?"

"That sounds amazing," Sergey said with a new level of energy in his voice.

"Excellent. That's exactly what I wanted to accomplish

today—to connect to your core career themes. We'll be building on these during the remainder of our work. We're off to a great start."

CORE CONCEPT

CORE CAREER THEMES

An individual's Core Career Themes are the most important elements they'd like to have in their career. These themes could include the day-to-day activities the person wants to pursue at work, the kind of environment they most prefer, the compensation level they're craving, and/or the values they prioritize most highly.

I believe that there are many potentially rewarding career paths for any one individual, which is why I like to begin by connecting people to broader ideas of what they most want in their career, rather than homing in on any given profession. Once a client and I work together to unearth these Core Career Themes, we distill the elements we've identified into a succinct list. This list serves as a touchstone for the remainder of our work, as it remains true even if a specific job we're exploring turns out to be a dud.

Here are three examples of actual clients' Core Career Themes.

Tanya's Themes
- healthy work environment
- opportunity to support others and improve lives
- emphasis on education and explaining concepts
- working with adults
- structure and organization
- relationships (as long as it's not all day)

Evan's Themes

- creativity and a sense of humor
- visually-oriented work
- goal-oriented environment
- quiet time and available space to create; time away from computer screen
- emphasis on excellence and practicing skills
- value placed on virtues like reliability, consistency, likeability

Carrie's Themes

- family, home, and community
- bearing witness to life passages for community (birth, marriage, death)
- radical work environment; an appreciation for looking at the world with an edgy perspective and challenging the status quo
- calming, healing energy, drawn to healing work, particularly women's health
- spirituality

LOOKOUT PART ONE!

The next section of exercises will guide you through the process of identifying your own career themes. Before you embark on this set of exercises, recognize the need for caution. There is one common pitfall that will render this work unhelpful and frustrating.

See if the following scenario resonates with you. If so, you'll want to circle back to the exercises in this section after completing the remainder of the book.

My client, Henry, and I had just gone through his pre-work questions. I'd asked him about a ton of thought-provoking and personal topics, and I was pleased to see his career themes coming into view.

Henry had a knack for networking, coupled with a fierce determination for matching individuals' skills to tasks at hand. He was a connector and was extremely personable with a service-oriented mindset. Though his background was in corporate sales, Henry spoke passionately about how much he cared for supporting underserved populations, particularly around the issue of food access. I was getting the distinct impression that he'd thrive in a nonprofit fundraising environment that dealt with his favorite cause. Towards the end of our conversation, I recounted my observations of Henry's career themes to him.

In most cases when I take the proactive step of bringing a client's apparent desires into greater focus, the response is positive: the client feels understood and has a sense of clarity about what they're looking for in their career. They feel hopeful and enthusiastic that we're on the right track.

Not Henry.

When I told Henry that I felt he had exceptional people skills, a clear gift for service-oriented work, and a determination that could help any kind of organization achieve its goals, Henry was less than thrilled. In fact, he sounded baffled.

"But what do I really want? What am I going to do next? I still don't see it," Henry said. His tone of voice contained a mix of apathy and a sense of defeat, as if he'd just run into a stone wall.

I took Henry's response in stride, as I'd seen it many times before. The issue was not that Henry's career themes were unclear. From my vantage point, Henry's desires for his career were in plain sight. The issue was that Henry couldn't see those themes . . . at all.

It was as though Henry was sitting in the front seat of a metaphorical car with his front windshield completely fogged up. Even though the road was right in front of him, his vision was blocked, so his pathway forward still felt obscured. That's why he sounded so disheartened and even a bit irritated by my comments. He was really *trying* to see, and had been for quite some time, but he wasn't having any success. And he wasn't going to be able to have success until we un-fogged his windshield.

If you've ever attempted to get insight into your career direction by reflecting on questions and repeatedly come away feeling discouraged and frustrated, take heart. The issue you're having is simply a matter of timing. Answering questions like, "What would I do if I had won the lottery?" can be helpful *if and only if* you're in a place where you can see the answers. If you aren't in that place, be kind to yourself and take the pressure off! Your first step is to un-fog your windshield. We need to clear out the things that are blocking your vision—things like doubt, assumptions, false beliefs, and possibly old pain from prior career decisions. Afterwards you can ask those reflection questions and move forward with much greater ease.

I explained the situation to Henry.

"We're going to spend a bit of time clearing out the things that have been obstructing your vision and limiting your perspective. Once we attend to that, we'll have much more success with the reflection process. It's just a matter of applying the right tools at the right time. We'll get this sorted out for you."

"OK, I think I see what you're saying. What I've been doing on my own certainly hasn't been working, so I'm game to give it a try," Henry said.

This time he sounded relieved. There was a bit of hope in his voice. He was finally getting the support he needed to make progress on his career direction.

LOOKOUT PART TWO!

I do want to offer one other word of caution regarding the exercises you're about to complete. It may be tempting to spend a lot of time ruminating over your answers to the following questions and then polishing your written responses. Let's face it: it's sort of enjoyable to think about yourself and what you like and don't like it.

Don't get caught in this mental place.

Give the questions below one to three hours of your time *tops*. Go with your gut instinct on your responses, and get through the questions. Once you've spent a few hours (at most) you should have about 50–75% of the picture. That's all we need at this point. The remaining portion is not going to be found in your head. It's unknown as of now and is going to be found as a result of engaging with the real world (which we'll discuss in the next chapter). Don't waste your time overthinking these questions.

EXERCISES

CHECK YOURSELF

Have you attempted answering questions about yourself (such as a personality test) in the past without success?

_____

Does identifying and thinking about your strengths and interests leave you frustrated and irritated?

_____

If so, please read the remainder of the book, emphasizing the exercises in Chapters 4–10, before attempting this chapter's exercises.

DIVE IN WORKSHEET

Fill out the following questions. These are not all easy, so give them a bit of thought. Remember, however, that your responses do NOT need to be perfect. If you find yourself getting stumped because of any one question, simply move on and finish the majority of the questionnaire. You may want to ask family and friends for some additional insights, if those people would be supportive and helpful in your reflection.

Education:

_____

_____

_____

_____

Professional Background:

_____

_____

_____

_____

Significant Achievements:

_____

_____

_____

_____

Most Recent Life Changes:

_____

_____

_____

_____

The result I want is...

_____

_____

_____

_____

_____

_____

1. Name five things you did as a kid that you loved and did well.

_____

_____

_____

_____

_____

2. Name five things you have done as an adult that you loved and did very well.

_____

_____

_____

_____

_____

3. Can you remember a time when you were working or playing and having so much fun that you lost track of time? Please describe.

_____

_____

_____

_____

_____

_____

4. What was so great about this experience? Can you pinpoint what it was that you enjoyed so much?

_____

_____

_____

_____

_____

5. What comes most easily to you? What are your superpowers?

_____

_____

_____

_____

_____

6. Do you notice that you do better or worse in any specific types of environments? (You could note social environment, physical environment, or anything else that seems relevant.)

_____

_____

_____

_____

_____

_____

7. What causes, if any, do you care most about? Why?

_____

_____

_____

_____

_____

_____

8. Name five activities that you actively dislike doing.

_____

_____

_____

_____

_____

9. What media do you regularly consume? For example, what specific blogs, magazines, newspaper sections, TV shows, or radio programs are you drawn to?

_____

_____

_____

_____

_____

10. What is the biggest dream that you gave up on?

_____

_____

_____

_____

_____

_____

11. What would your greatest dream be if you knew you could not fail?

_____

_____

_____

_____

_____

12. What do other people always say about you? Who are you to others?

_____

_____

_____

_____

_____

_____

13. What are you tired of putting up with?

_____

_____

_____

_____

_____

14. What would bring more meaning to your life?

_____

_____

_____

_____

_____

_____

15. Who do you want to be in your life? (Answer this how you feel—there is no required format.)

_____

_____

_____

_____

_____

16. What is your natural mode of taking action? Are you a Quickstart, someone who moves quickly into real world action? Are you a Fact Finder, someone who does a lot of research before acting? Are you a Follow-Thru, someone who

enjoys working within and creating structure? Are you an Implementor, someone who uses physical objects to understand the world? (These conative styles are from Kathy Kolbe's research and work.)

_____

_____

THEMES

Once you've made a solid effort at completing this initial set of questions, you'll want to go through one more time by yourself, with a friend, or with a coach to identify your Core Career Themes. (If you decide to go the route of working with a friend or coach, you'll want to choose someone who is non-judgmental and open to unexpected possibilities.)

Consider each of the following sub-questions for the original questions. Either jot down some quick notes or talk through each of these points. Look for places where your hands start flying or the energy in your voice picks up. As you probably already know, our energy levels can be psychological signals—so be mindful of these fluctuations.

Education

Note what influenced your educational choices. Sometimes people simply fall into a particular major in college. Other times people choose their academic path with a lot of intentionality and planning. Why did you choose the course of studies that you took? Did you enjoy your coursework? Are there any memorable projects or activities you participated in that stand out to you? What other majors did you consider?

Achievements

Were your achievements more meaningful to you or to the outside world? Did you enjoy them?

Professional Background

Of the jobs you've held, what elements have you most liked? What have you most disliked?

Questions 1–5

For each response, ask yourself "why?" For instance: *Why* did I enjoy that activity so much? Try to break down the components of the activity to isolate the different elements.

For example, if you loved organizing spur of the moment plays with neighborhood kids when you were a child, what was it that most drew you to this activity? Get specific. Was it being in charge? The freedom of creative expression? The thrill of getting attention when your troupe performed? Break down your different experiences into their underlying parts.

As you skim through the ideas present in your responses, where do you notice you feel the most energy and enthusiasm?

What common themes appear to be present? These could be subjects, activities, environments, or types of people that you are particularly drawn to.

Question 6

Is there an element here that is non-negotiable? For example, do you need to have a day where you get to interact with people to feel fulfilled?

Question 7

Do any of these causes exert a strong enough pull on you to take them beyond a "hobby" level interest?

Question 8

Again, we're looking for non-negotiables. Is there anything that we absolutely need to avoid in discussing your future career (such as high-pressure deadlines or boring, monotonous filing)?

Question 9

What I'm most interested in here is that which goes beyond just entertainment. Are you reading a ton about a specific subject, like biking or writing or cooking in your spare time? We want to pay attention to the areas that you're intrinsically drawn to, the ones where you might not even realize that you're putting a lot of time and effort into them. We want to pay particular attention to a subject that has the potential to go beyond a hobby-level interest.

Question 10

Is there any juice left in this dream? What drew you to it in the first place? Why did you stop pursuing it?

Questions 11–16

What do your responses to these questions say about your priorities and your character?

Now distill this wealth of internal knowledge into just a few core themes. Include the items that are most important to you, the skills and strengths that you exhibit, and the areas of interest that fascinate you. Jot these themes down in the space below. Note anything that seems relevant at this stage.

THEMES:

_____

_____

_____

_____

_____

_____

_____

_____

_____

_____

_____

Now look at the Core Career Themes you've identified above, and narrow down the list to the most important elements. We're looking for five to ten items. For example, you may have listed travel as something you love. Consider whether each item is truly a critical element to a future job, or simply a nice benefit. There is a difference, so honor that, and then write your winnowed down list below.

MOST IMPORTANT THEMES:

_____

_____

_____

_____

_____

COACH'S NOTE

Great work! I know it takes effort to dig into the above questions. We're now mostly done with the introspective part of this work. We'll be taking the gold mine of information you just uncovered with us on our journey together and will continue to refine your clarity as we go along.

I realize that you may still feel unsatisfied with the lack of specificity at this stage in your journey. That's natural, and it's OK to acknowledge that discomfort. I often tell clients to imagine that the whole universe of career options is a big sphere. Notice that while you may feel like things are still vague, you have narrowed down your choices to a wedge of the sphere, which is a tremendous start.

For example, you may know for sure that you want to do work that allows you to spend at least some time outdoors. Look at that: you've just eliminated all strict office jobs. It's perfectly alright to feel fuzzy about the precise job title you want to be looking for at this point. You may also be beginning to feel nervous about how you will find a job in your particular sphere. It's okay not to know this yet. This first step is meant to identify your general section of the sphere. That's all.

In my experience, identifying a general area of career interest is actually quite easy to accomplish. It's the next bit—

zeroing in on a more narrow focus and gaining momentum in a new direction—that takes the most effort. As I mentioned earlier, this last degree of clarity is not going to be figured out by thinking about it more. Check out the following career myth to see what I mean and to get a hint of the upcoming steps in the process.

CAREER MYTH: YOU CAN THINK YOUR WAY TO YOUR CALLING

Amber decided that she wanted to be a paleontologist shortly after a grade school field trip to a museum.

During that trip, she watched with utter fascination as a visiting lecturer described the process of uncovering fossils to better understand other eras of life on earth. Her young imagination was captured; it was at that moment that Amber latched onto her dream career of becoming a paleontologist.

In the aftermath of this realization, Amber found herself making frequent library trips and filling her backpack with books about fossils and science. From there, she sought out a summer internship with an environmental consulting firm, and eventually earned a master's degree in Geology.

You probably know someone like Amber—someone who had a moment of clear conviction regarding their chosen career path in grade school or college. These people march around with such certainty toward their desired destination that it may leave you wondering, "Why don't I have a calling like that?"

So, with the best of intentions, you set out to find your career answer. You started taking tests, hoping to find an answer. You may have kept a journal or made an Excel spread-sheet about potential graduate school programs. You talked to your family. You meditated. You made a vision board. You journaled some more. All to no avail. What gives?

Could it be that you've been falling for a career myth?

THE CAREER MYTH

In my work, one of the most common myths I encounter is this belief that we each have a calling residing deep within the recesses of our psyches.

People tend to think that if they could only master the correct sequence of mental jujitsu moves, they'd be able to unlock the door to a magical dream career that resolves all of their doubts and insecurities.

Attached to this unrealistic viewpoint, people then become fixated on finding the right method of accessing their core essence and desires. And when these methods don't work, people get anxious and stumped. They stall out and wind up putting their half-formed insights to the side in frustration. Weeks later they try again, and the cycle repeats.

We fall prey to the myth that it's possible to find our best career path through introspection for a couple of reasons.

We see people like Amber, who seem to have found their perfect place in the world by tapping into magical inner knowledge, and we expect the same for ourselves. Plus, when we take actions that feel proactive, such as filling out career, personality, or aptitude tests, we give ourselves the feeling of making progress, even though these gestures of self-inquiry typically don't actually challenge us to do anything in the real world. And finally, introspection and dreaming are fun to do, at least initially. It's nice to spend time in the safety of our own brains, considering possibilities or dreams without exposing ourselves to any sort of failure or rejection.

WHAT'S REALLY GOING ON

How would you react if I told you that you'd be able to figure out the name, character, and physical appearance of a future best friend or significant other? The only preparation you'd need in order to do this would be to think about it long enough. My guess is that you'd probably laugh, because the idea is ridiculous.

Sure, you might be able to give me a list of some traits that you'd like to see in a good friend. You could possibly guess a common name. There's a chance you might even know that person right now, and based on some past interactions, you could hazard the guess that your relationship has the potential to grow and deepen.

But there's also a chance that you don't know who this future friend is because you haven't met them yet. Thinking about it isn't going to get you closer to knowing them. Actually participating in life, showing up, and meeting people is what will do the trick.

This same idea applies to figuring out your career direction. You must be willing to take action and try new things. You have to give yourself the opportunity to "meet" a career path that catches your eye, as exploring is more about action than thinking.

It's unlikely that your mind already knows about the tremendous multitude of career possibilities present in the world. How could you? For that reason, it would be foolish to spend too much time mining your own mind. You would be much better served by interacting with new people and experiences to broaden your horizons.

YOUR CALLING IS INSIDE YOU . . . WELL SORT OF

When I work with clients, I always tell them that we will begin our work with a bit of introspection. Any successful career change is the result of choices informed by preferences, dreams, strengths, interests, and values. In this way, it makes sense to begin with an assessment of those areas. But I always frame this initial work by explaining to my clients that we can do this reflective work relatively quickly. Efficiency is essential: we can get in, get the information we need, and then get out. Lingering too long in introspection leads to spinning in circles and getting stalled out by confusion.

My clients and I spend much of our time together working to determine ways for them to build on their self-awareness through new experiences. They might talk to people in a field they're considering, take a college class on a relevant topic, attend a conference, or pick up a side project. By taking action, my clients are able to arm themselves with new information and real world data points. They're able to gain clarity about the type of work they're considering.

They can learn whether or not the field they're thinking about actually matches up with their pre-conceived notion. They can check their interest level after spending more time interacting with their chosen work. And they often learn of a new opportunity that they'd never heard of before because they've taken a few small steps in the direction of their interests.

Time and again, I've seen people make the most progress when they combine their knowledge of themselves with real world actions. If you think back to Amber's story, you'll notice that the idea of being a paleontologist didn't just drop into her head out the blue. It came to her because she had an authentic emotional reaction to her experience when she was on a field trip—out in the world. Being present in a new place was all it took for this particular profession to catch her eye.

Do yourself a favor: Get out of your head and take some field trips of your own. Choose experiences that match up with what you're interested in or what you're dreaming about. That's the way to find the career path you're looking for.

Now that you are armed with an initial idea of what you want next in your career, it's time to look at the big picture process of how to move from that idea to reality. The next chapter will give you a clearer sense of how career changes actually happen.

Chapter 3

UNDERSTANDING THE CAREER DIRECTION FORMULA

As I mentioned in the last chapter, one of the hardest things about navigating a career crossroads is dealing with all the doubts, fears, and other mindset issues that go along with making changes. Before we dig into strategies for working through these areas, I want to present you with a high-level overview of the different aspects of moving through a career crossroads. To give you a sense of the big picture, I'll tell you the story of my client, Rama. From there, we'll dig into the nitty-gritty of how people get stuck (and how to get unstuck) in Chapters Four–Ten.

My client, Rama, presented me with a pretty straightforward case. I want to use her story as a way to illustrate what the career transition process looks like with relatively few hiccups so that you'll have a big picture understanding of what steps you'll be taking next.

Of course, knowing the steps of a career transition and living through these steps are quite different. Sure, the steps may be easy to understand, but the execution of them can be daunting. Our thoughts, fears, and social environments can enable us to wallow in a state of inaction, particularly if we don't have the right tools to maneuver through these common challenges. The remainder of the book will teach you what you need to know to get out of your own way so that you can get on your way.

Rama reached out to me because she was fed up with the dysfunction of her current work environment, but lacked a clear vision for what she should do next with her career. She was a conscientious and thoughtful woman in her late twenties living in Boulder, Colorado. She had a strong desire to make changes in her life, but didn't know what to do next. Rama and I worked together through my Just Get Me Pointed in the Right Direction program, a shorter-term coaching program designed to provide clients with the support and guidance necessary to figure out their next career steps, along with accountability around making a change. Rama was an ideal candidate for this program precisely because her case did not have any especially complicated or confounding factors.

As I got to know Rama, it quickly became clear to me that she was naturally drawn to organization and structure. During our initial conversations, she gleefully recounted childhood memories of spending time by herself organizing her belongings. She told me how she used to entertain herself by scrambling all the books in her room and re-alphabetizing her bookshelf. As an adult, she inevitably found herself making procedures and setting up systems to bring calm to chaos in every single job she'd ever held, no matter what the job description entailed. She had an acute eye for detail, truly got pleasure out of organizing and planning, and believed in doing work to benefit the larger community. She was most interested in finding a job that would increase the level of Fulfillment she felt on a day-to-day basis.

Rama's current job as a program manager for a financial aid organization had some elements that she enjoyed. She valued the fact that her work genuinely had potential for positively impacting others, even if community engagement wasn't explicitly part of her role. However, shoddy management and dissatisfaction among other staff members compromised Rama's morale. She found herself questioning if she was doing the right thing with her career for the long-term.

Together, Rama and I worked to identify her Core Career Themes. From there, I instructed her on how to complete the process of career exploration. I asked her to look through a site that aggregated information on different career options to find a couple jobs that appealed to her. (Details on this exercise are in Chapter 8.) Unsurprisingly, Rama came back with a list of community-oriented jobs ranging from managing a nursing home to organizing programming at a community center to creating a financial literacy curriculum for public schools.

Rama and I talked over all of her ideas, and I noticed that she became most excited and energized when talking about her research about curriculum design, particularly in the field of personal finances.

"Why is this area so interesting to you?" I asked Rama.

"I've seen people in my family struggle with their finances and with developing a basic understanding of how to take care of themselves. It's so important to teach kids how to care for their own well-being, so that they can grow up to be successful adults. Plus, I like the idea of creating a structured curriculum, where everything has its place," she explained.

"I totally see it. Designing financial curricula sounds like a job that hits on a lot of important areas for you. We'll use this as your lead career hypothesis, which is basically our best guess as to what you'd like to be doing next," I explained. "But before diving into this career path right away, I'd like you to explore it a bit more. Talk to people in the field. Attend industry events. Do anything else that can help you get closer to a real world experience of what this job would actually entail on a daily basis," I instructed.

Rama got to work right away. She immediately recognized the difference I was trying to highlight between researching a potentially ideal job and exploring feasible career options and their daily responsibilities. Rama used her alumni network to learn from people who were working in curriculum design. In addition to reaching out to people in the field, she gathered information about job prospects and typical education requirements for the role. Rama also did her best to get a sense of what day-to-day life would feel like while working in this field. When Rama learned of an industry conference, she made it a point to attend.

As Rama moved forward with these productive exploratory steps, I monitored her reactions. Each time I checked in on a recent experience, Rama sounded enthusiastic and interested in the work. The more she learned, the more confident she felt that she was on the right track.

Rama and I discussed a more detailed plan to help her transition into this field. One thing Rama had learned was that pursuing a graduate degree in the field of Family and Consumer Science would boost her chances of getting hired by a school system. So Rama began researching graduate schools in her desired field. Even though graduate school was on the horizon, there was still the more immediate issue of Rama's current toxic work environment.

Rama and I developed a short-term plan for her to transition into an interim community-oriented job (one that didn't require a master's degree), which would allow her to get more experience in this possible career path while she prepared for admittance into graduate school. Our longer-term plan was for her to attend graduate school and land a financial literacy curriculum position within the public school system.

With her eyes on these concrete goals, Rama began developing her network to support her job search. She joined an industry association with a local chapter and took on a leadership role within the organization, which introduced her to many new people with whom she could foster connection and an ongoing dialogue. At the same time, she actively reached out to her existing network to let people know the types of jobs she was looking for. After interviewing for several positions, Rama chose to work for a particular program that encouraged community members to reduce their level of credit card debt. At her new workplace, Rama had an amazingly supportive boss, which made Rama's day-to-day much more pleasant. The new job would serve as a wonderful bridge to the ultimate destination Rama had in mind.

Throughout the process, Rama remained persistent and patient. She was determined to make a successful career change. She stuck with it and is now happily preparing to attend graduate school while spending her workweek in a much better work environment.

CORE CONCEPT

The Career Change formula steps are not that complicated, but there are a bunch of places where people get tripped up along the way. Here's a high level overview of the steps involved in making a career change.

1. Make a career hypothesis.
2. Test out your hypothesis.
3. Monitor your reaction.
4. Develop connections.
5. Boost your credentials/prep your job search materials.
6. Begin your job search.
7. Keep at it until you get it, while being flexible.

Sounds easy enough, right? Not so fast! While these are the necessary steps for you to think about before you can go about sorting out your career direction, the actual *implementation* of these steps tends to be quite challenging. In fact, many people find themselves getting the most stuck right at the beginning. Sometimes people get stuck because they believe career myths. Other times they get stuck due to a mindset issue, or a simple misunderstanding of what actions will be most helpful to them.

Before jumping into the steps of the Career Change Formula, let's assess where you are likely to get stuck. That way, you'll be able to focus on the relevant chapters of the book that will be most helpful to you.

LOOKOUT!

Going through a successful career change can be extremely rewarding. However, there are always costs to making a switch, even if it's just leaving one job to go to another. You will most likely lose the social capital that you've build in your current career path. You may have to start over with building a network. Many people experience a (hopefully temporary) financial dip when they decide to make a move. There can also be associated schooling and credentialing costs associated with making a career change. The good news is that your prior work experience and life skills will likely help you to get through this dip and rebuild faster than you did in your previous career choice. Just a heads up that this dip is part of the process and doesn't mean you're doing anything wrong.

EXERCISES

CAREER DIRECTION QUIZ

Do you find yourself saying things like the following statements when asked about what's next for your career?

"I don't know."

"I feel trapped."

"I'm just so stuck."

"I'm frozen."

"I don't feel confident enough."

"I'm at a loss."

"I don't know the right choice."

"I'm not sure."

"I can't seem to move forward."

"It feels hopeless."

"What I want is too far away."

"It's complicated."

"I really don't know."

"I can't decide."

If so, did you notice something about all of these statements?

I'll give you a hint: these phrases are primarily describing symptoms of a problem. But until you identify the actual issue, you'll be unable to move forward. It's like going to a doctor with the symptom of a severe headache. The doctor would look beyond the symptom to try to identify the cause of the symptom to then prescribe an appropriate treatment. We want to do the same thing with your specific career case.

If you could make a diagnosis of what was *causing* your career issues, I know you would get to work on fixing it.

Unfortunately, you're stuck between a rock and a hard place. You know something is in your way, but your lack of knowledge of what that "something" is keeps you stalled out day after day, year after year.

This quiz is a cheat sheet to help you figure out what the symptoms you're experiencing mean.

You'll answer a set of 31 questions and tally your responses.

Then you'll pull back the curtain on what's really going on by diagnosing which of the *10 Categories of Stuckness* you fall into.

Once you know what's behind your feelings of confusion around your career direction you'll be better situated to get on your way.

Get started by circling any of the statements below that describe your situation. Interpret your results by matching up your responses with the *10 Categories of Stuckness* at the end of the quiz. You may fall into more than one category. That's okay. Just knowing what's going on is a step in the right direction.

1. I have no idea what I want.

2. I enjoy the work I do generally, but my current job is making me rethink everything.

3. I have a pretty good hunch as to what I'd like to do next, but I haven't taken any action on moving towards it.

4. I want to leave my industry altogether, but it feels like such a huge leap.

5. I worry whether I'm good enough or qualified for the work I'd most like to do.

6. I'm disappointed that the last career move I made didn't turn out the way I'd hoped.

7. The people around me are pretty negative whenever I share my career ideas. They point out all the potential flaws, and I get discouraged.

8. I feel a lot of fear when it comes to making career decisions.

9. I don't feel appreciated for contributions I make in my current job. What I provide and what my company is looking

for don't seem to match.

10. Many career ideas look appealing, but I find it hard to know what would be a good fit for me.

11. I have a lot of self-doubts and worry about whether or not I'm making the right career choices.

12. I spend tons of time online looking at job ads.

13. I reached a career goal that I thought I wanted, but it isn't attractive anymore.

14. I told someone what I really wanted to do. They told me it wasn't possible. So I stopped trying.

15. I can't figure out how to balance my urgent need to leave my job with my longer-term desire to switch careers completely.

16. I feel stuck and confused.

17. The level of social interaction at my current job isn't to my liking.

18. I'm sending out resumes left and right, but getting no responses.

19. I'm frightened about what will happen if I try something new and unknown.

20. I don't know what to focus on with my job search.

21. I don't have a clear sense of my strengths and interests or how they could relate to a career path.

22. The amount of conflict and disorganization at my job is getting under my skin.

23. I want high pay, a great lifestyle, and work that lights me up, and I'm frustrated that I can't find it.

24. I know exactly what would make the people in my life happy, but I feel less clear about what I really want.

25. I have a dream that's close to my heart, but I'm extremely hesitant to give it a go.

26. Lots of people in my life have strong opinions about what I should be doing that differ from my own ideas.

27. I don't know what jobs are out there.

28. I get scared and freeze or I get scared and distract myself with taking care of other responsibilities whenever I think about my next career move.

29. I've looked at so many job descriptions that my head is completely spun around. I don't know what I'm even looking for anymore.

30. For years I thought I wanted one thing. Now I'm starting to want something different.

31. I have a clear idea of what I don't like, but I'm not sure what I *do* like.

Score your results by matching up your responses with the categories below to diagnose what's keeping you stuck. I've included a high level note on what you'll need to do to move through each type of stuckness and will go into much more detail on how to handle each of these situations in the remainder of the book.

10 CATEGORIES OF STUCKNESS

1) Lack of Experience - **1, 10, 31**
   You may be new to the workforce. Or you may have lots of work history, but no experience with work that matches up with what you most want. In both cases, there's a trick here: devote some time to career exploration. However, I'll warn you that "I don't knows" are often a socially acceptable masquerade for a different category of stuckness. If you fall into this category, plus some of the others, you'll want to start with addressing the other issues first.

2) Environmental Factors at Work - **2, 9, 17, 22**
   You dislike your current job, but it sounds like it's not the job itself that's bothering you. It's the environment. Dig deeper into this realization by trying to identify what your ideal environment might look like.

3) Sounding-Board Needed - **20, 21, 27**
   Over the years, I've seen one category of client that mainly just needs to talk things through with a non-directive, compassionate witness who can be supportive and help them flesh out their vision. Of course, it's essential to be careful when choosing the person with whom you share your ideas. But it's a good idea for you to bounce your thoughts off someone else to get things moving.

4) Dying Dream Scenario - **6, 13, 30**
   This scenario isn't talked about much in the career-advice space, but it's a real situation that I've seen many people face. When you've worked hard for a dream only

to realize it's not where you really want to be, there are a lot of emotional ramifications. Realize this is a big deal! Be sure to process what you're leaving behind so that you can move forward with an unburdened heart. See Chapter 4.

5) Mindset - **3, 5, 11, 16**

Lots of things are going on in your head, including a whole slew of unhelpful thought patterns. Our thoughts can create false barriers that block us from moving forward. That is, unless we become aware of their hold and practice re-routing them in a more productive direction. Start by noticing what thoughts are holding you back the most. Talk them over with a trusted confidant to tease out some new ideas or try to find a new, more helpful perspective on your own. See Chapters 5 and 10.

6) Short-Term / Long-Term Confusion - **4, 15**

You don't need to a hit a home run with your next career move. You might hit a single, like getting out of a terrible job, but staying in an ill-fitting industry. From there you'll be in a better position to make your next move. Just because you can't reach a long-term goal immediately doesn't mean you should totally drop that goal. Work towards your big dream with short-term goals. See Chapter 6.

7) Social Environment - **7, 14, 24, 26**

Here's a wakeup call: we're social creatures, and the support (or lack of support) you receive from the people around you can make or break you. I'm not saying you should cut ties with anyone in your life who isn't a proactive cheerleader, but I am saying that cultivating the presence of supportive people and messages in your life needs to be a conscious choice. By the same token, it is harmful to spend time with people who bring you down. See Chapter 7.

8) Lost in Job Searching - **12, 18, 29**
I know you're trying to work on your career, but spending oodles of time on the online job boards is actually counterproductive. They'll leave you muddled, discouraged, and worn out. Step away from the computer and invest your time in building and main-taining your network instead. As I'm sure you know from other areas of life, talking to people face-to-face is often much more rewarding than diving into a virtual rabbit hole. See Chapter 8.

9) Fear - **8, 19, 25, 28**
Career decisions are life-altering, so it's natural that they bring up a lot of fears. Instead of letting your fears dictate your actions, try to connect to the reason *why* you are seeking change, and take small steps toward that outcome. See Chapter 9.

10) Over the Moon Expectations - **23**
I see this most often in younger professionals. Look: it's totally possible to get the big three—high compen-sation, amazing lifestyle, and fulfilling, stimulating work. However, most jobs are higher in some of these areas and lower in others, particularly when you're first starting out. Holding out for perfection today will keep you from putting in the effort you need to exert to build your dream life. Compromise doesn't mean admitting failure. It means you can finally get going. See Chapter 5.

List your main areas of stuckness below.

_____

_____

_____

_____

_____

COACH'S NOTE

Does this process seem overwhelming? It can take some work, but hang in there! Note that I gave you a great deal of information all at once in order to show you the full landscape of where we're going in our work together. In reality, however, we only need to take things one step at a time. I'll be guiding you along throughout the rest of the book—so you don't have to go it alone. If you'd like further help with breaking down the steps of your career transition, go to www.cardycareer-coaching.com/bookgift and sign up for the Step-By-Step Career Change E-Course. I'll help you to stay on track with weekly emails that will guide you through the process and encourage to keep your spirits up as you go.

I also provide professional career coaching services and would be happy to support you further.

If you fell into Categories 1–3, 6, 8, or 10 on the Career Direction Quiz, my Just Get Me Pointed in the Right Direction career coaching program will be the right fit for your situation. This program provides you with devoted time, attention, and accountability to make progress on your career. It is best for folks who aren't sure which way to go, but know once they connect to that direction they'll be able to follow-through on moving towards it without much resistance.

If you fell into categories 4, 5, 7, or 9 on the Career Direction Quiz, consider my Career Direction Clarity + Action Plan or my Phoenix Rising coaching programs. If a car is stuck in the mud, it requires a bit of extra work to dig it out. The same is true if you find yourself to be very stuck with your career direction. It will take additional time and concerted effort to wiggle things loose so that you can get moving again. These programs provide more in-depth support to set you free to move forward. The Career Direction Clarity + Action Plan program is focused solely on improving career. The Phoenix Rising program is for strong people who have been through a rough time and want to do a more comprehensive rebuild of their lives.

You can learn more about all of my coaching programs at: www.cardycareercoaching.com/coaching.

CAREER MYTH: YOU CAN HAVE IT ALL

I find that there are two main influencing voices in the realm of career decisions.

One voice is the "Practical Parent". This voice will advise you to avoid risks. Choose a stable and predictable industry. Bring home the bacon, and make sure you're doing so consistently.

The second voice is the "Passion Police". This voice demands that you find your passion. Do what you love. Don't just put your time and talent toward any old thing. Instead, do something you really care about and enjoy.

Both of these voices focus on what you'll get if you listen to them.

Security and wealth.

Passion and purpose.

Unfortunately, neither voice ever communicates the fact that ANY career choice you make will also have consequences. Sure, this sounds obvious—but most of us overlook this inevitable fact when we get caught up in clinging to practical anxieties, or when we become lost in fantasies of fulfilling a singularly fulfilling life purpose.

Maybe your secure 9 to 5 government job comes with a lot of bureaucracy and boredom. Or your high-income job comes with a correspondingly high level of stress and a constant feeling of being "on". Perhaps your passion job isn't earning quite as much as you would have hoped, or your ascent to success is taking longer than you'd like.

Take a look at the areas of job satisfaction below. Which elements are present in your work? Which are lacking?

Income

Job Security

Reasonable Hours

Work Boundaries (e.g. work stays at work)

Challenge

Intrinsic Motivation and Enjoyment

Comfortable Environment

Collegial Atmosphere

Benefits (Health Savings Account, Retirement Matching, Paid Vacation)

Freedom

Community Involvement

Appreciation from Superiors

Community Benefits (e.g. work makes a positive impact on others)

Physical Health (e.g. you have enough time and energy for self-care)

Flexibility

Work / Family Balance

Does anybody have all of these elements in their job? While it's completely possible, I imagine most of us achieve a portion of these work satisfaction areas and sacrifice a few as well, particularly when we're in those initial steps of building our careers.

And that's OK.

In fact, I mention these consequences because acknowledging the full effects of our choices can be empowering.

For example, knowing that a high-stress job is taking a toll on your health might mean you find proactive ways to cope and shift the balance a bit. Perhaps you take luxurious, unplugged vacations whenever you get the chance. Or maybe you've realized that your passion pursuit is still in its infancy, which means that you decide to take another job to fill in financially while you learn how to bring your dream to life.

Whatever you choose, and whatever corresponding consequences come along for the ride, can be dealt with productively. It's comes down to deciding what you're willing to put up with. You can always change your Career Strategy choice and try something different down the road.

In the remaining chapters, we'll go over the most common areas where people get stuck in more detail. Take each section one by one, but focus on the sections that strike you as most relevant to your situation.

Chapter 4

OVERCOMING PAST
CAREER CHALLENGES

Getting knocked down and worn out is part of being human. Tough life circumstances arise at times, and they can affect our ability to move forward. In this chapter, you'll read a story about Maggie, a client who went through a particularly challenging situation of working to achieve a childhood dream—only to realize it had turned into a nightmare. Alongside this instructional story, you'll also learn the key ingredients for cultivating resilience in the aftermath of a troubling event in your life or career. We must identify and address these issues thoughtfully before charging into action. Reading this chapter can be your powerful first step in moving forward.

Maggie reached out to me during a not-so-great time in her life. I could tell that it had taken a lot of courage for her to acknowledge her own need to ask for help and share her situation. She was in the midst of a major funk about her career and her life's path in general. She felt stuck and couldn't see a path to something better.

Maggie had grown up in a "foodie" family. Family vacations centered around what restaurants they would get to try. As a child, she'd seen the focus and elegance of chefs at top tier restaurants and thought to herself, "That's where I want to be." There was never any doubt in her mind that she would become a chef.

Maggie initially learned to cook from her father, whose favorite hobby was experimenting in the kitchen. By the time she was a sophomore in high school, she had cooked her way through every cookbook in her family's home (and there were many).

With intense determination, Maggie earned a scholarship to a top cooking school in France. She performed well and enjoyed her coursework. Upon graduating, her chutzpah and talent garnered her a position at a world-renowned restaurant in New York. For almost eight years, Maggie fought her way through the daily grind of food prep, long hours, and customer complaints.

Unfortunately, time in the kitchen began to take a toll. Maggie routinely worked 12–14 hours a day, six days a week. She was on her feet for the majority of that time—always in hot kitchens, facing unending deadlines. The restaurant she had worked so hard to be a part of turned out to have a rigid hierarchical structure, meaning there was little room for growth or upward mobility. The pay was nothing to write home about, and her social life and health were suffering from the demanding schedule and work conditions. Above all, Maggie was just plain exhausted.

One day, Maggie hit a breaking point. She called her family and told them she couldn't take it anymore. With their support, she quit her job and moved back in with her parents in North Carolina.

By the time she called me, Maggie had gotten some rest, and her energy was beginning to return to a normal level. But that didn't make her situation much better. She was thoroughly disheartened that the dream she had worked so hard to fulfill had turned out to be a nightmare. For years, being a top tier chef had been the central focus of her life. Without that identity, Maggie felt lost and rootless.

In addition, Maggie was plagued with self-doubt. She had been so certain that being a chef was the right career path for her. How could she trust her intuition a second time when the first time had turned out so poorly? Maggie was also particularly worried about being "behind" her peers. At 34, she had no significant other, no job prospects, and no clue what to do next.

While the details of Maggie's situation were unique, her case presented a predicament I had actually seen many times before.

The word "career" sounds impersonal and professional, but in actuality all careers are laden with meanings and feelings. The career choices we make and the work environments where we spend our time can have a huge effect on our well-being. They can diminish our self-confidence. They can wear us down. They can leave us feeling incompetent, neglected, or embarrassed.

I've had clients who staked their heart on a career, like Maggie, only to become disillusioned and self-conscious when they find that their dream didn't work out. Not only must these individuals grapple with the disappointment of a dead-end career path, but they also often find themselves worrying about how friends or family may perceive their "inability" to make it work.

I've had clients who have worked in dysfunctional work environments. They've told me horror stories of staplers and names flying across office spaces. Other clients have been thrown into crisis-like situations under poor managers. Work becomes a high stress exercise in putting out a perpetual fire. Others have faced inhuman expectations that deplete their ability to ever feel successful, no matter how hard they work.

These types of career paths and work environments invariably lead to burnout—especially when combined with my clients' dedication to their work. Other areas of my clients' lives—family, health, and general well-being—suffer neglect under the strain of the intensity of the demands of their work. These clients usually come away from their work experiences with a number of scars and a few lingering emotional wounds. It's in this weakened state that they face the daunting task of picking up the pieces of their lives.

The common thread among these stories is that something in the client's work history has negatively impacted them and affected their ability to move forward.

In Maggie's case, we needed to attend to her history before we could move on to her future. Maggie signed up for my Phoenix Rising program. This particular program is designed for people just like Maggie—strong, capable individuals with a fighting spirit, who have gotten knocked down by life in some way and want to improve their lives in a major way. Through this program, my clients and I work together over an extended period of time to pick up the pieces of shattered confidence to rebuild their careers and lives even better than they were before.

As you may have guessed, it became clear that Maggie was

shifting her career strategy from pure Fulfillment to valuing a job that provided her with a combo of Personal Well-Being and Financial Security.

During my first few conversations with Maggie, I worked to help her clean out the emotional pain that she had endured. The process simply involved having Maggie share her story with me while I listened with compassion, paying particular attention to the emotional impact of what she'd been through.

For example, I asked Maggie to tell me about how the restaurant had impacted her personally.

"Every day was so stressful. I felt like I was always under scrutiny," she told me. "It's really hard on your body to stand in a kitchen all day too. I'd work through aches and pains. Burns. Cuts too. At the end of the day I'd come home from work and just collapse into bed. I'd be lucky if I had enough energy to shower before hitting the sack. Then I'd wake up the next day to my alarm and do it all over again. On my day off I tried to take care of errands, but some days I just plopped on the couch. So I didn't have much of a personal life at all outside of one or two friends I'd made at work."

"Sounds brutal!" I told Maggie, particularly affected by her description of struggling with both emotional exhaustion and physical pain at work.

"You know, I was so busy when I was working there that I never even questioned the schedule—well, not until the very end," she continued. "I thought that was just the way things were. It was OK for a while. And then I totally ran out of gas." Maggie sighed. "I see that the life I had working at that restaurant was really crazy now that I'm talking about it. Very unbalanced."

"I see that too," I told Maggie, making sure that she felt

heard and understood.

When Maggie told me that the straw that broke the camel's back was when a new manager with an unforgiving attitude towards mistakes came on board, I reflected back, "You felt incredibly frustrated because you were working so hard and couldn't ever seem to do a good enough job."

"Yes! It no longer seemed worth it. I kept asking myself, *What am I even doing this for anyway?*" Maggie replied.

We didn't dig through every detail, but we talked through the emotionally-charged areas. There were naturally a few tears shed as she told me her story. Maggie felt heard, and benefitted from hearing an objective perspective on her situation.

I find that people often perceive their career struggles as personal failings, when in actuality they are simply reacting to environments that would wear most anyone down. Recognizing that they had a natural human response to a tough situation tends to relieve a good portion of the client's suffering, and allows them to begin moving forward.

Once I felt that we had uncovered the big pieces of what she had been through, I guided Maggie through a mini-meditation focusing on the cultivation of compassion.

"What we need to do to continue the process of moving through this is to pay attention to forgiveness. I want you to bring the wisest, kindest, most compassionate part of yourself to mind. From the viewpoint of this kind self, I want you to look back on Maggie over the past eight years or so as she made career decisions and struggled through the restaurant work. And I want you to try, as best you can, to offer her forgiveness for anything she did or didn't do. In your mind's eye offer her compassion and reassurance. Treat her with the same love you would treat a friend who had just gone through a rough time or a child who needed comforting. I'm going to be quiet for a few minutes while you give it a go."

I waited for Maggie to have a chance to do this important work.

"OK, wrap up what you're thinking. How was it?"

Maggie let out a long sigh.

"It was pretty emotional. I didn't realize how much I'd been holding onto there. I'm crying again," Maggie said ruefully.

"That's a-OK. Crying is actually what we want here. And what did your wiser self tell Maggie from the past few years?"

Maggie sniffed.

"Just that she'd been doing the best she could. That it was going to be OK. That I'm proud of her, and she's stronger than she realizes."

"Excellent work. And, yes, you did an incredible job over those years. You were in an extremely competitive and tough environment, and you showed up day after day and performed."

"I think I've been really hard on myself about what I *didn't* do over those years. I didn't mean to neglect my health or social life, but that's what wound up happening. So part of what I did during that meditation was to try to forgive myself for the areas I missed over the past eight years. And I tried to let myself know that I would pay attention to them now," Maggie told me.

"Great. You might want to do this meditation a couple more times in the coming days. It doesn't have to be any big thing. Just a few minutes to forgive yourself for being human and having a rough patch. If you get stuck, just think about what you would say to a friend who had gone through a similar experience," I instructed.

"Thank you. I will."

Maggie's life and career hadn't turned out the way she'd thought. Like many of my clients, she needed to acknowledge what had happened and allow herself to feel compassion for those events. We can't change the past, but we can process it to provide ourselves the opportunity to learn and move on from it.

Sometimes our good intentions with our careers don't take us exactly where we want to be going, but that doesn't mean that they weren't important impulses or that we did something horribly wrong. It just means it's time for a course correction based on a new, deeper understanding of what we need and what we need to avoid.

CORE CONCEPTS

A PSYCHOLOGICAL BANDAGE

As we go through life and make career decisions, there are lots of opportunities for us to get hurt or off track. When these things happen, it's important to tend to them. Much like you would clean and bandage a physical wound in the presence of a skilled medical professional, we need to clean and dress any emotional wounds that we've endured with the appropriate help.

All you'll need to do to complete this step is to find a compassionate, trustworthy witness (coach, therapist, friend, or family member) with whom you can share your story. You're looking for someone who will give you caring attention and simply hear what you've gone through. Sometimes it takes a couple tries to find the right fit. Take your time getting to know someone (if you're connecting with a professional), and make sure you have a solid rapport before sharing your story.

If you've been through a work experience that has left you struggling with your confidence, burnt out, or discouraged, you'll likely want to take the time to address and come to terms with the events that have happened in the past by talking them over with someone else. Processing what has occurred will help you to move forward.

FORGIVENESS

Recognizing that we're all human and that we all make mistakes is powerful medicine in and of itself. Offering yourself forgiveness and compassion for what has happened will help you to let go of the past so that you can move more fully into the future.

LOOKOUT!

Maggie's experiences and wounds were fairly fresh in her mind when she came to me. As such, it made sense to start our work together by addressing what she had been through. However, there are many other cases in which re-hashing the past is unproductive.

In these cases, the events have often taken place further back in the client's history, and the client has had ample time and opportunity to talk through their situation already. When telling their stories, these clients tend to sound like they are recounting a familiar fairy tale. They know all the highs and lows of the story and are looking for a response to what they went through. On my end, I usually feel bored.

While discussing a tough period is generally a healthy step in moving on from the past, it can become counterproductive if you dwell on it too much. Tell your story once or twice, and then let it go. We don't want to re-hash prior events over and over again, as this will stall your forward movement.

One way to tell whether you need to share your story or not is to see if the wound feels fresh. When you think about the events do you feel emotional? This emotional charge should begin to diminish once you've told your story. If the events happened a long time ago, and you've already told your story to a number of compassionate audiences, then skip this step. It's time to move on.

While the events may have lost their emotional charge, it's possible that you've internalized unhelpful beliefs from past events. In this case you'll want to focus on the material in Chapter 5 to make forward progress. Specifically consider what you've made your prior experience mean about yourself, your capabilities, or your future.

EXERCISES

SHARE WITH A COMPASSIONATE AUDIENCE

This exercise is for anyone who has been through a tough stretch at work where you've been hurt.

Steps

1) Find a non-judgmental person with whom you feel comfortable. This could be a therapist, coach, friend, or family member.

2) Give yourself a bit of time to get to know the person (if it's not a friend or family member). See if you still feel comfortable with them and want to open up about what you've been through. If you do, move on to the next steps. If not, go back to the first step.

3) Tell this person your story. You will likely feel emotions as you do this. Let these feelings come up and pass through you. The emotions are not going to hurt you or overwhelm you. They will come and then go. Hang in there.

4) Feel compassion for yourself.

5) Notice that you feel a bit lighter and more relieved for having spoken about what you've been through and how it impacted you.

FORGIVENESS MEDITATION

Bring your wisest, kindest self to mind. Then call to mind a difficult time in your life and take a look at yourself at this time with this loving presence. Send your old self some love and compassion. Offer him or her forgiveness for anything he or she did or didn't do. Let him or her know that they'll make it through. Sit with him or her and give them comfort.

LENGTHEN YOUR PERSPECTIVE

Oddly enough, many times really amazing things in our lives come from our worst moments. Consider something that you appreciate in your life right now or valued in the past. Write it down. Now think about what not so great event played a role in your attainment of this good thing. Write it below.

_____

_____

_____

_____

_____

_____

_____

If you're up to it, try to imagine what positive outcome might possibly flow from your current situation. Fill it in below.

_____

_____

_____

_____

_____

_____

_____

COACH'S NOTE

Undergoing difficult experiences, such as a career struggle, can often make us lose perspective. All of our attention and energy gets funneled into the emotions around the event or situation that we've just been through. However, it's important to remember that our lives always extend beyond any one experience, no matter how all-consuming that experience may seem in the moment. Even if it feels impossible, it's helpful to remember that taking a longer view is available to you at any moment. Just because one job or project didn't go the way that you wanted does not mean that your career is doomed forever. It only means that one thing didn't work out the way you'd hoped.

Recognize that life extends beyond any one event. And in fact, we can learn and grow the most from those things that don't go the way we plan. We can use those lessons to do a better job the next time around. A career misstep means you're one step closer to figuring out what will really work. Give yourself a pat on the back for making it through this experience, forgive yourself for any mistakes, and get ready to lace up your boots. We're about to give this thing another go.

CAREER MYTH: CAREERS ARE UNEMOTIONAL, BUTTON UPPED AFFAIRS THAT STEADILY GROW ONE STEP AFTER THE OTHER

Have you ever worked really hard for something that didn't work out?

Maybe it was a golden job opportunity. You made it to the final round of interviews, but you didn't get the job. Or perhaps that side project you'd been working on for months didn't receive the recognition that you'd hoped for. Or maybe you gave your all to a project at work that completely tanked.

The result? You felt disappointed, rejected, or hurt—painful emotions that most of us generally try to avoid.

One of my most vivid experiences of work related heartbreak occurred one Sunday afternoon. I'd worked diligently over the prior weeks to prepare for a program launch. I had high hopes and expectations for the results I'd achieve. I even made sure to get feedback in advance to make sure that things were looking good and that I was on track to hit my goals.

I promoted my offering all week. And with each passing day I felt more worried. I lost some sleep. No one was buying. Everything came to a head that Sunday afternoon, the last day of my promotional efforts.

I was out with my husband on a beautiful day walking around a new and interesting part of town. But the sunshine and the good company were completely lost on me. I was in a terrific funk. Everything seemed hopeless, and I felt like total crap. I couldn't get over the news that my work hadn't worked out. My husband attempted to help me see the bright side, but I struggled to see it. I was in an emotional thunderstorm that left me feeling ragged and raw.

And then, after a few days, the storm cloud I was under passed. I returned to work. I got on with my life and my business. After several months I launched again, with additional support, more knowledge, and much better results.

When we put our hearts into something, when we really care, there will always be the potential for heartbreak. Heartbreak certainly isn't something that I'd choose to sign up for every day of the week. It's unpleasant to go through tough feelings. But every now and again I think it's healthy to step up in a bigger way, to put ourselves on the line, and if necessary, endure the pain of things not going our way.

We're capable of surviving tough emotional states. Unpleasant feelings pass through us like weather systems. They don't last forever.

Stretching ourselves—and yes, enduring some heartbreak—helps us grow stronger. We learn that feelings are temporary. We can step back and maintain a sense of perspective, knowing that this too shall pass. Ultimately, any of us can learn that the pain we feel upon stepping out of our comfort zone is short-lived. It's intense, but it ends. I'd much prefer that sort of pain to the perpetual feeling of disappointment and regret that comes from never trying.

If you've had a heartbreak recently, take heart. Have

courage. Lick your wounds and get back up. Try again. You're strong enough to make it through.

The next chapter covers one of the most universal areas where people get stuck when considering a career change—their heads! Our assumptions, projections, and beliefs can dramatically skew our sense of possibility, leaving us discouraged or at a loss. With greater awareness we can see through these false barriers and move forward more easily.

Chapter 5

SEEING NEW POSSIBILITIES

---

*Many people unconsciously hold onto beliefs
that block their ability to see new possibilities.
My client, Mason, ran into this problem with his
career, resulting in a lot of career angst. While
Mason's situation is unique, I chose to tell his story
because it succinctly and powerfully illustrates how
we can all be blind to the limitations we create
in our own minds. With the help of another set
of eyes, it becomes much easier to both identify
and overcome these false barriers. See if you can
relate to the concepts presented here, if not the
specifics of Mason's circumstances.*

My client, Mason, is a passionate, energetic man in his late twenties living in London, England. For the previous decade, he'd put all his professional energy into cultivating his career as an actor. He worked with the best acting teachers. He had professional headshots and a website with a couple of demo reels. He auditioned regularly.

When I asked him why he was so drawn to acting, he answered that it had been an important part of his life for as long as he could remember.

"I've been acting since I was a little kid. I was a total ham back then. I think I naturally enjoyed the attention that being on stage gave me," he began. "Then in grade school, the appeal became more about the opportunity to be part of a team, to do something fun together. All my high school friends were either actors or part of stage crew, so we spent a ton of time together. As I got older, I really got into the craft of acting, figuring out how to develop a character and digging into understanding the storyline. Acting is just fascinating to me. I love pretty much every part of it." Mason spoke quickly and enthusiastically. It was apparent that he had figured out work that he loved to do and was committed to pursuing it.

There was just one problem. Mason had only gotten occasional gigs from all of his efforts, which usually didn't pay very much. If you looked at Mason's career from the outside, including the way he presented himself on his website and on social media, you'd have assumed he was killing it. There were photos of him and celebrities, him on the red carpet, and lots of upbeat updates about how wonderfully things were going for him. In reality, Mason came from a wealthy family, and he relied heavily on his parents for financial support as he pursued this dream.

Mason reached out to me because he was questioning his commitment to acting. He signed up for my Career Direction Clarity + Action Plan program because he recognized he needed support around his mindset (something that takes additional time) in order to get unstuck.

"I know I'm supposed to follow my passion, which acting very clearly is," Mason explained to me with self-awareness and clarity. "But sometimes I wonder if it's worth it. Here I am, 28 years old, and still going to my parents for money," he continued with a sigh. "I guess what's really putting me in a tough spot is the fact that I met this awesome woman. I could see us getting married one day. But I just can't imagine taking things any further with her when I couldn't even buy her a ring with my own money, much less provide for a family. I want to be able to do those things, and it sucks that I can't. I feel stuck."

Mason was a capable individual, but his financial situation was indeed stunted, severely so, due to the mutually reinforcing combination of an infamously low-paying career path and the generosity of his parents. Furthermore, the fact that he was still holding onto his parents' purse strings led to family drama. He couldn't create the emotional boundaries he wanted to in order to establish a healthy separation from his parents because he was financially dependent on them.

"So what have you been thinking about doing next?" I asked.

"My family is always suggesting I go into sales," he answered with resignation. "I'm clearly a people person, and I don't really like sitting at a desk. So that's an option. I've considered the restaurant business too. There was one day where I thought running a bed and breakfast would be kinda cool. But everything other than acting feels like selling out. I don't want to give up on all the work I've already put into this path, and I don't want to let down all of the people who have supported me in the process, either."

As I got to know Mason, it became apparent that he felt torn between two ideals: his desire to continue pursuing a dream career, and his deep, equivalently valid, wish for financial independence. He believed he needed to choose between career fulfillment on one end and money on the other. He also thought that making one choice would mean completely sacrificing the other. Because of his extreme mindset, neither choice was particularly appealing. So he held on to his decision to pursue his acting career, all the while feeling disappointed by the financial consequences of his choice.

A few of the statements Mason made as he explained his situation to me really caught my attention.

"I'm supposed to follow my passion at all costs."

"I have to choose between acting and making money."

"Earning money from another source means I'm giving up on my dream."

I could tell that these thoughts were impeding Mason's ability to see possibilities in between the all-or-nothing extremes he'd been considering.

"Mason, the thoughts that we have frame our perception and influence the possibilities we're able to see. I often think of it like this. Imagine that career options are like a bunch of doorways around a big room. Certain thoughts can close those metaphorical doors, and keep us from seeing alternative pathways forward. I'm going to take you through an exercise in which we open one of those closed doors," I explained. "Once that door has been opened, I will encourage you to recognize that it is your choice as to whether or not you will walk through it. You may choose to pass up that path, but the goal is for you to realize that you have more choices than you think. Does that make sense?" I asked Mason.

"Sure. How does this exercise work?" Mason replied.

"We're going to examine one of your limiting thoughts. The first step is to identify the thought and zero in on it with conscious attention. Doing this helps us realize how many ideas typically float around in the back of our minds without our realizing it. After we identify a thought, we'll look at the impact of the thought. And finally, we'll consider alternative perspectives, and think about the impact of creating this freedom," I explained.

"Sounds good," Mason said.

"One of the things I heard you say earlier was that 'Earning money from another job means I'm giving up on acting,'" I mentioned. "Is that thought a peaceful or stressful one for you?" I knew that reflecting back to Mason what he had said to me would invite him to consider the impact of his thought patterns.

"It's stressful. I don't want to give up on my dream."

"What is the impact of this thought- 'Earning money from another job means I'm giving up on acting'? In other words, how do you feel when you think it? What does it make you want to do or not do?"

"I feel disappointed, but also stubborn. I don't want to give up on acting, so I feel myself dig in my heels and resolve to just stick with it. I don't let myself even consider other jobs. The impact is that I stay stuck, right where I am."

"Nice work. Now we're going to look for a different perspective, something that's more helpful. What's another way of looking at picking up another job?"

Mason paused for a moment. "I have no idea."

"That's OK. What we're doing here is like a mental workout. It's meant to be challenging. Just for the sake of the exercise, why could picking up a job and a paycheck be a good thing, rather than something that dashes your dreams?"

"Well, I might be more confident. I'd probably feel proud of myself for being better able to take care of myself."

"Sure. What else?"

"Hmm, well, there's that saying that when you want something done, give it to a busy person. Maybe if I had more structure to my days, I'd be more productive than when I was just booking acting gigs and trying to network."

"Interesting thought. Can you see any other reasons why having another gig might actually boost your acting career?"

"Well, a lot of landing parts is about who you know. So maybe I'd meet new people who might help me down the road."

"Could be. So if the initial thought was, 'Earning money from another job means I'm giving up on acting', what's a new thought about this topic? We're looking for one sentence."

"Working another job could *help* me with my acting career."

"Tell me how that could be true again."

"If I think that the job will support me with acting, everything feels different. I can now see that if I had another gig going on, I'd end up feeling more focused on acting when I did have spare time. That it would mean getting to know more people and being more proactive. I think I'd feel more like a responsible adult. I'd be able to take care of myself. That would be amazing."

"It would help you a lot with the financial independence you're after too," I added, affirming the idea I had sensed Mason picking up on.

"As we've been talking, I'm realizing that my income-earning muscle feels pretty weak. I think it would feel good to exercise it, to make it stronger. I know I'd feel better if I wasn't so reliant on my parents."

"How was that exercise for you?" I inquired once we had finished up.

"It was really interesting. People have been telling me for *ages* to try getting a job, but I always thought it was, as you said, an all-or-nothing choice. Acting versus having another job. I hated the idea of that choice. I never thought of it the way we just did before—that a job could actually help me with acting. I feel a little less stuck," Mason explained.

The remainder of Mason's work with me involved helping him to identify a job with enough flexibility to permit him to maintain his focus on his audition schedule. The job also needed to be something that was compelling enough for him, as he has a dynamic personality and a strong sense of what he likes and doesn't like to do. Of course, we discussed that whatever he would do probably wouldn't be as engaging as acting, but we could still shoot for something better than a dreadful day-to-day. Mason was in the process of maneuvering from a pure Fulfillment focus to a Fulfillment and Financial Health focus.

Mason wound up taking a flexible sales position for a growing plumbing business. Interestingly enough, when the company president learned Mason was an actor, he cast Mason as the voice and look of their radio and television advertising campaigns. In the midst of all this, Mason is still working independently on his acting career, as it's something he truly loves and he has no plan of giving up. Surprisingly for him, but unsurprisingly for me, Mason has simultaneously become more and more stimulated by his sales and marketing job, and is happily building his very own nest egg.

My goal is always to support my clients in their process of getting what they most want. In Mason's case, he wanted to pursue acting, and he wanted to be financially independent. His belief that it was either one or the other prevented him from seeing other possibilities and kept him stuck. Taking on an extra job helped him move forward. It helped him create a schedule that provided his life with more structure, and it was a solid step towards his long-term goal of becoming financially independent from his family. (This option is not a universal answer—it's just what worked for Mason based on what was important to him at that moment in his life.)

Other clients have gotten tripped up by becoming attached to other ideas that keep them from seeing the real life possibility of what they're really wanting.

Ollie thought that her household (of five kids) would fall to shambles if she ever went back to work, so she spent year after year longingly entertaining the possibility of a career in her mind, without ever taking any real world steps towards re-entering the workforce. Ollie and I had to question her assumption that things would fall apart at home without her constant attention. We looked for examples of how her household could survive without her presence. It turned out that two of her kids were already out of the house and the other three were well-adjusted, independent kids in middle and high school. When I probed more, I discovered that there were certain tasks that were meaningful to her in relation to her family, and others that she didn't like. We talked about how she could be there for her kids to make them feel loved and supported, while also keeping herself in mind. We discussed how she could keep doing her favorite parenting and home-making tasks, while learning to ask for help in the other areas. This prioritization allowed Ollie to free herself up to re-enter the workforce, and created a greater sense of balance between caretaking and taking care of herself.

Alyssa believed that she had to earn a six-figure salary straight out of college. Yet her career themes pointed in the direction of public service work. As long as she held the belief that it was a necessity to earn a large paycheck, she would be unable to see the possibility of a career path that actually appealed to her for reasons other than compensation. She wound up holding onto the same crummy job she'd held all through college while waiting to figure out what she really wanted. Alyssa needed evidence that she could move forward and experience a sense of progress in her career without a hefty salary. I had her make a budget of her bare bones living expenses so she could be completely aware of the practical necessities at hand. After completing this exercise, Alyssa realized she could support herself doing the work she actually wanted to do. She felt liberated to move forward.

George was quite certain that the true definition of success was that of his ambitious, career ladder-climbing friends, even though he preferred a slower pace of life. He never let himself get close to career paths that fit his personality because he knew they would be at odds with "success." George and I talked a lot about his own personal definition of success and how it was okay that it was different than his peers. Once he felt more comfortable with what he wanted, George was able to act on his true wishes.

Byron worried that the time he took off work to tend to a family matter meant that he was spoiled goods, even though he was a highly-educated, hardworking individual. As long as he held this belief, his ability to take action and cultivate persistence to land his next job was compromised. Once Byron and I questioned his belief that his career was doomed, he was able to feel more hopeful and optimistic about reconnecting with former colleagues. He began taking the actions that would help him with re-connecting with his career.

For each of these clients, the issue was not that they didn't know what they wanted. It was that a thought they'd created or picked up prevented them from taking action. Until their beliefs were brought to their conscious attention and challenged, these thoughts were in the driver's seat of the client's lives, dictating their feelings and behaviors.

CORE CONCEPT

Our thoughts and beliefs influence how we feel and how we behave. Many times these ideas can lurk in the background of our minds, influencing our behavior without our conscious minds catching on. By identifying, questioning, and addressing these limiting beliefs, we are able to move forward more freely, with a greater sense of empowerment and intentionality. This is a powerful concept that has been effective in many of the cases that I've dealt with. The specific thoughts clients hold vary greatly, but the underlying methodology works for any limiting belief. My understanding of thoughtwork has been greatly influenced by the work of Byron Katie and Brooke Castillo.

There are two times when working on our thoughts (I call this "thoughtwork") can be a highly effective exercise. The first is when you notice yourself totally stalling out on taking any action at all. The second is when you feel crummy. In both instances, taking a pause to notice what you're thinking underneath the inaction or unpleasant feelings can be a game-changing tactic. When you give yourself the space and time to look critically but compassionately at your thoughts, you can provide your brain with helpful alternatives that will support your forward progress.

Keep in mind that our goal is not to clear out every limiting thought you've ever had. That would be impossible! Instead, try to imagine your thoughts like a brick wall in front of you. In order to see through to the other side of the wall, you don't need a bulldozer. You just need to knock out a few bricks to give yourself a window to the other side. Then once you've knocked out several of the bricks, there will be room for you to actually move through the wall and into greater possibilities.

When I work with clients, I ask them to take as much action as they're able to in a given moment. When they find themselves getting stuck, we take a look at the thoughts that may be causing them to procrastinate and stay stuck. These two types of work behave like pistons. Actions move the client forward as much as they can. Clearing out limiting ideas then creates space in which even more action can be taken.

LOOKOUT!

Once you learn this framework, it may be tempting to spend a lot of time just looking at your thoughts and trying to improve your thinking patterns. While this tool is extremely helpful, and particularly illuminating in the immediate aftermath of learning it, it is not a cure-all. You'll still need to keep an eye on taking action. You'll still need to draw on your courage and cultivate resilience as you challenge yourself to act beyond fear. Making a career change involves discomfort, plain and simple. This tool will help to remove some unnecessary discomfort, but it will not eradicate all the uncertainty or challenging feelings that will come up during the process.

EXERCISES

WARM UP THOUGHTWORK EXERCISE

When I'm out speaking, I often have my audiences do this warm-up exercise to illustrate the concept of thoughtwork.

Take a moment to imagine that I have a magic-wand that will grant you a two-week, all expenses paid vacation to anywhere in the world. This trip has been cleared with your boss. All your responsibilities at home will be handled in your absence. You can bring (or not bring) anyone you like on this trip.

Where would you go on your vacation?

Now close your eyes for a minute or two and imagine that you are actually on that vacation. Bring this trip as fully to life in your mind's eye as you can. Get creative, and try to tap into the powers of your imagination as much as you can. Consider what you feel, what you hear, what you see, what you smell, and what you might eat. Notice how your state of mind changes as you do this exercise.

When I'm guiding an audience through this exercise, I stay quiet for a few minutes and then have the participants open their eyes as I ask them this question, "How many of you are feeling better now than you did when you walked in the room?" Normally half to three quarters of the room raise their hand and express that they're feeling notably better.

Then I ask the audience, "Why? What changed?"

The answer? Nothing has changed in their lives other than where I directed their focused attention during that brief minute or two. In all likelihood, the concerns of the day took a backseat as they imagined their enjoyable vacation. Putting their brain on this task brought up positive feelings. Our thoughts about ourselves, our capabilities, and the possibilities in our lives also generate feelings, just as this imaginative exercise did.

THOUGHTWORK

Are you stalling out on taking action or feeling disheartened about your career?

If so, take five minutes to write down the thoughts that come up as you imagine moving forward. For example, if you've been meaning to edit your resume for months, but never get around to it, imagine you are about to pull up your resume. However, instead of working on it, jot down the thoughts that come to your mind.

_____

_____

_____

_____

_____

_____

_____

_____

_____

_____

_____

_____

Read through the thoughts that you've articulated. Put a star next to the thought that feels most limiting to you.

Re-write the thought here:

_____

_____

_____

Is this thought peaceful or stressful? Is it helpful or limiting? (Only move forward to the next question if it is stressful or limiting. If it's not, pick a different thought to use in this exercise.)

_____

_____

How does the thought affect you? How do you feel and behave while thinking this thought?

_____

_____

_____

_____

_____

_____

How would your life be different if this thought were not present in your life?

_____

_____

_____

_____

Now jot down three to five alternate perspectives on the situation. This is like a mental workout. You're looking for new viewpoints. At this stage, it doesn't matter if the new perspectives totally resonate with you or not. One way to get started is to consider opposites to the original thought. For example, if the original thought was "No one will hire me," some opposites could be "Someone will hire me" or "No one will fire me." Play around with how you express the thought and the possible opposites until you land on three to five new ways of looking at things. Write them below.

_____

_____

_____

_____

_____

_____

_____

_____

Read through the ideas you've listed, and put a star by the two perspectives that resonate the most with you.

Re-write these two thoughts here:

_____

_____

_____

_____

_____

Now think of three specific examples of why (or how) these new thoughts could be true. For example, the new thought "Someone will hire me" could be true because it's happened in the past, because there are forgiving employers, or because you're putting a lot of effort into your job search.

_____

_____

_____

_____

_____

_____

_____

Now write one small action that you could take while keeping these new possibilities in mind. This doesn't have to be anything huge. In fact, for many people finding a small, concrete task to complete is relieving. For example, you could edit your address on your resume and save it as a new version. List your action step below.

_____

_____

_____

_____

Voila! Traction gained.

Continue to take small actions until you get stuck. Then repeat the above thoughtwork exercise to clear more space for yourself.

MAKE THE POSITIVE ARGUMENT

In any situation, we can adopt multiple perspectives with which to consider and understand our circumstances. If asked, you would be able to present an argument that supported any viewpoint. As you begin your career exploration, I'll be asking you to focus on making the positive argument (just for now!). This means asking yourself why things will go well, why this career path will be a good fit, and so on. This will keep the window of possibility open long enough for you to explore a particular path.

Why could the career path you're considering be a good fit?

Why could it work out well for you?

Why are you going to be successful with your career change?

Jot down some answers below, along with any other questions that lead your brain in a positive direction.

_____

_____

_____

_____

_____

_____

_____

_____

COACH'S NOTE

If you're having trouble coming up with alternative perspectives on your own, try asking a sympathetic friend, coach, or therapist to assist you by putting their brain on the task. We can become so enmeshed in our own way of seeing things that it can be hard to be open to other possibilities. A fresh set of eyes can be just what's needed to have a breakthrough.

My Career Direction Clarity + Action Plan and Phoenix Rising programs will be the best fit for you if you notice that your thoughts are wedging you into a corner. These programs contain extended coaching time to help you work through your sticking points. You can learn more about these programs at www.cardycareercoaching.com/coaching.

CAREER MYTH: YOU CAN DO ANYTHING!

Sometimes the thoughts we think may sound positive, but are actually detrimental. Here's an example.

The other day, an acquaintance began telling me about her younger brother. He's an Ivy League graduate—clearly very motivated and bright—but he has no clue about what he wants to be doing with his life.

"He's still trying to figure out what he wants to be when he grows up," she explained. "Everyone keeps telling him that he can do anything." She shrugged, "He's having a hard time."

Oddly enough, this message that her brother was receiving—"You can do anything"—is incredibly stressful. It's a common piece of advice, and a seemingly empowering one. But I see that it is a total non-starter for most people.

Why?

It's quite simple: if you could actually do anything, wouldn't you choose a Nobel prize winning, million dollar making, socially prestigious path that forever changes the world for the better and puts your name in the history books? Of course you would. And how are you supposed to know how to choose a path like that?

People who hear and believe this hyperbolic piece of advice struggle because it carries them to such a lofty and abstract place. It's as though they are reaching up and trying to hold firmly onto a cloud. Their hand goes right through and comes up empty. Anything? How do I choose what to do out of anything?

When we are looking to make a change in our careers, there needs to be a clear vision of what the change could look like in sight, even if that sight is in your imagination. You need to be able to grab onto a metaphorical anchor, something that interests you, holds meaning, or helps you achieve your goals. From that place you will have a much better chance of actually getting started.

Recognize that your ideal career path may not lead to saving the entire world or you becoming the richest person on a Forbes list of wealthy elite. Not many people experience those kinds of history-making outcomes—and that's OK. Your unique life is waiting for you. Start by grabbing onto an anchor goal and get started.

This chapter focused on the role our mindset plays in the process of making changes in our lives and our careers. With the anecdotes I chose, I began hinting at the fact that our financial health is intimately linked to our career choices. This is an essential thing to recognize and one that some of us tend to avoid thinking about. The next chapter digs deeper into this important subject.

Chapter 6

HONORING YOUR FINANCIAL HEALTH

The question of what career path you're on, or want to be on, is directly tied to your financial health. In other words, there are very practical stakes at hand when it comes to making a career change, which is often what makes this such a scary topic for people. But here's the thing: money is neither the most important thing in the world, nor the least. It is simply a factor to consider responsibly and integrate into our career decisions thoughtfully. In the previous chapter, I began addressing the issue of financial priorities, as I told the story about the actor Mason. In this chapter, I tell the story of my client, Tom's, reckoning with his financial priorities. Neither Tom's story nor Mason's story demonstrates a universal answer to the question of how any one of us should go about addressing the role of money in our career choices. My intention is simply to show the range of possibilities that are available. Our financial sensibilities are extremely personal, and we need to get in touch with what matters to us before we can make any big decisions. We also need to consider the lives we affect, primarily our family members, with the choices we make.

For my entire career I've had a company car and a cell phone plan. As the years have gone on, I've built to a really decent salary. It's hard to imagine giving that all up. Not to mention that I've got a wife, and we're thinking of starting a family soon. Making money is the biggest thing that's keeping me from leaving my job," my client, Tom, explained.

Tom and I had recently begun working together in my Just Get Me Pointed in the Right Direction program. He wanted support and focused guidance about the steps he needed to take in order to improve his career. Tom knew he wanted to leave his job on some level, but didn't know exactly why or what alternatives he was looking for. He was most concerned with increasing his sense of Fulfillment and with reducing his stress (Personal Well-Being).

Tom had been working for more than a decade as an in-house lawyer for a large corporation in Washington, DC. Tom's work hours were challenging and overwhelming. His department was under-staffed and over-stretched. Tom was also bored with the day-to-day at work. He had spoken to me several times about how burnt out he felt and how eager he was to consider moving on to a new field.

By working through my process, Tom quickly homed in on the career path he most wanted—that of a social media manager for a mid-to-large-sized brand. While Tom had gained clarity about what he wanted to do, resistance came up for him as we began discussing the necessary aspects of a potential action plan.

There was a pretty simple issue behind his resistance: money.

Whenever Tom did consider a new job, he looked at one thing: the salary. And when he did so, he was almost inevitably disappointed. While he didn't love his current job, he did value the steady, sizable paycheck and the stability it provided to him and his wife, especially as they discussed the (exciting, but anxiety-producing) potential of starting a family.

"I can't tell you how many times I think about leaving in any given week," Tom admitted to me. "But there's just one thing that keeps me hanging on—the paycheck. Otherwise, I would have been out of here yesterday."

For Tom to move forward, he would need to do two things. First, he'd need to broaden his definition of what career "success" looked like. As long as he understood the worth of his job solely in terms of salary, he'd stay stuck—either on his current path with which he was dissatisfied—or perhaps doing something else equally unfulfilling, just for a steady income.

Second, he'd need to approach the topic of finances in general with a more thoughtful and careful eye. Currently, Tom was fixated on a particular way of thinking about income and financial health. This was leading him to approach the topic of finances with an impulsive, knee jerk reaction.

"What's the price of your paycheck in terms of the rest of your life?" I asked Tom.

"Well, there are a lot of costs. I'm short-tempered with my wife when I get home, so there's pressure on my marriage. I used to be fairly athletic, but that's pretty much gone out the window. I've lost touch with most of my friends, and have gotten used to living in this place of perpetual burnout. It even affects my work—sometimes I'll procrastinate on projects because I'm just so tired of it all," Tom described.

"Sounds like your job impacts your life a lot," I replied.

"My job *is* my life," Tom said with a little chuckle. "And I don't like my job, so that's the big problem."

Financial compensation is the most quantifiable element of a job, but it's far from the only thing that matters when it comes to thinking about a career path. To illustrate this point concretely, I asked Tom to consider his quality of life as another measurement of his job—to get him thinking about the broader implications of his work. While the compensation at his job was high, the day-to-day cost of his job was also high—his relationship with his wife, his health, his social life, his overall well-being, and even his work, were all suffering.

Tom and I had previously discussed how he might go about getting a job as a social media manager for a brand or company, where he could exhibit his creativity and his people skills. In his (limited) spare time, Tom had amassed a sizeable following on Twitter, and he loved learning about how to better connect and collaborate with others over virtual platforms.

"Imagine you're working as a social media manager of a company," I advised Tom. "I know you've already spoken to a few people in the field. What would the compensation and the quality of life factors look like in this new job?"

"From the people that I talked to, it sounded like the compensation would be a lot lower than what I'm currently making. The size of my paycheck would likely depend on how many people I had working under me. Small team, smaller paycheck. Big team, bigger paycheck. There'd be the new factor of being 'on call' a lot more too. But the stress level overall seems to be a lot lower. Plus, social media interests me content-wise. I love relationship building and crafting messages that will resonate with a large audience. So in that sense, I think the day to day would be more enjoyable," Tom described.

"What about your health, and ability to find more free time for yourself?" I asked.

"The job is basically a 9–5 position, though I would still need to keep my phone by me even when I'm off work. My evenings would be a lot more flexible, so I could probably get back into running again, which would improve my stress level and health. Gosh, that would be really nice," Tom continued, thinking things through.

"I want you to compare two possibilities, just for experimentation. Imagine where you would be in your life in 30 years if you stayed as an in-house lawyer versus if you moved to working as a social media manager. I realize that there are a lot of possibilities in between those two extremes, and a lot of possibilities even within those two options. But try just describing to me what you envision at both ends of the spectrum," I instructed.

"Oof," Tom said with a chuckle. "That's a really good question. If I stayed on the course I'm on now, my health would keep getting neglected. My home life might not be so hot because I'd be completely worn out by the time I got home each night. My connection to friends and things outside of work would be weak. I wouldn't like my life very much, but my bank account would be in great shape. I know that I would be able to provide for my family monetarily—but I'm not sure how involved I would get to be as a spouse or parent, since I'd be working a lot."

"What about the other extreme? What would happen if you left today and began working as a social media manager?" I probed.

"In that scenario, I imagine that my life would be a whole lot better. Like I said before, I'd have time to run, which is something I haven't been able to do regularly since law school.

I could spend time with my family and cultivate friendships. If my experience running my personal Twitter account is any indication of the work itself, then I'd probably be way more engaged, and actually like what I was doing," Tom described.

"And financially?"

"Well, there would be less to write home about. We might not get to take as many vacations or go out to eat as often. Now I can buy whatever I want without thinking about it. But if I earned less, I'd probably need to be more attentive to my budget, especially for the sake of my family. My savings would be lower, which would be hard. My wife works, so that helps, but we might really have to make some changes," Tom said.

"So let's start to think about it this way: there isn't a right or wrong answer here. There's just your answer. What feels like the right choice for you?" I asked Tom. "Keep in mind that you can look at this through the 'short term versus long term' lens. For example, you could work for another decade as a lawyer, build a solid nest egg, and *then* leave. Or you might decide to hold onto your in-house job for one or two more years to sock away some savings for your family and then make the switch over a longer time horizon. Or it might be time to make the switch right now," I explained, trying to offer some reassurance as well as practical advice.

"As you say that, the idea of building toward a change is what resonates with me. I can hold out here for a little bit longer. Maybe my wife and I could practice living on a reduced budget, and we could save the excess. Just saying that feels good, because it acknowledges the financial piece that I've been worried about, while also showing me that I don't have to stay in this job forever," Tom reflected with a palpable sense of relief. "Earning the money at the price of my quality of life is not something I want to do. So in that sense, I know I definitely want to leave. But I like the idea of being strategic about it," Tom explained.

"That sounds great. So the next thing to do is to take some time this week to look at your finances. I want you to figure out what you need financially—at a bare minimum level—to be satisfied with your life. Really focus on needs here, and pull out all the 'wants'. Look at the implications of staying at your current job for one or two years, and see what you'd be able to swing financially. The overall idea here is that we want you to face your financial priority head on, and address what taking a salary cut would actually mean for you and your family. Then you can figure out how to make it work," I instructed.

"OK," Tom replied. "I think that I've been focusing on salary as the only consideration when thinking about different job possibilities, like you were saying. But it's more than that. I'm realizing that some people might be good with the lawyer lifestyle. It's just not for me. I'll sit down with my wife this weekend and take a look at our finances."

"And remember too, there's always a financial cost to making a change. But it's unlikely that whatever salary you go to next is going to be the salary you have in five years," I reminded Tom. "So recognize that some of the financial dip is temporary—and look at what you can handle."

"Yup. Got it," Tom replied.

After looking at his finances, Tom made an exit plan from his current job. He decided to stay for at least one more year, so that he could focus on building his savings and learn to manage his budget better prior to the transition. He also decided to focus on developing contacts in the social media marketing world by attending events and conferences, and reaching out for some coffee dates. Tom told me that having a plan and a goal to work towards made a huge difference in how he felt day to day at work.

"It's still draining and stressful to be at work," Tom admitted. "But now I know it's not forever—and that alone is a tremendous relief. I see my savings account going up bit by bit, which I know is going to help my family, so that alleviates the financial worries I've had about making a change. And I feel good about putting in a bit of extra time towards developing my social media contacts. It feels like I'm finally making progress, where for so long I just felt stuck. I'm really grateful for your help. I couldn't see my way out on my own."

CORE CONCEPT

CAREER SEESAW

Here's a quick question for you:

Why are air traffic controllers consistently ranked as one of the highest-paid professions?

There are a few simple reasons. It's because the job:

- has a high barrier to entry;
- entails an intense level of responsibility—people's lives are at stake;
- involves focused attention; and
- is very stressful.

Imagine I asked a room of people, "Hey, want to sit in a dark room staring at little dots on a computer screen, knowing that every decision you make could affect hundreds of people's survival?"

I'd suppose that they would answer, "No thanks. That doesn't sound like such a great gig."

Yet society has an urgent need for this profession.

Imagine that, in addition to the aforementioned proposal, I added, "You'll get paid six figures to do this job."

Suddenly, more hands shoot up with interest, right? That would certainly be my educated guess.

Pay is called compensation for a reason. It *compensates* for the not-so-great aspects of jobs.

Other less-than-pleasant aspects of high-paying jobs can include crazy hours, being on-call, or a large upfront investment of time and money.

There's a flipside here.

When a given job has more inherently enjoyable aspects, there is less of a need for society to incentivize people to go after it with money.

Instead much of the compensation lies in the job itself.

These more pleasant jobs may include "perks" like:

- low stress;
- opportunity for creativity and self-expression;
- people or community oriented;
- low barrier to entry; and
- predictable or flexible schedule.

This kind of lifestyle can wind up being less expensive, quite literally. Think about it: when life itself is pretty enjoyable, we all feel less of a need to spend money on indulgent experiences or luxury objects. Plus, there are reduced physical and psychological symptoms of chronic stress, so fewer trips to the doctor, the masseuse, or the five-star resort are needed for regular rejuvenation.

There are absolutely people who work in a lower quality of life, higher-paid profession that love what they do, take pride in their work, and find a lot of meaning in it. As I mentioned, these priorities vary from person to person.

And there are also people who work in a higher quality of life, lower-paid profession that get crafty and wind up making boku money. (There are also jobs that stink and don't pay well too.)

But I just wanted to point out this general trend for you. There's a career seesaw out there. As quality of life goes down, pay goes up. And as quality of life goes up, pay goes down.

Which type of job should you choose? There's no judgment in my question. It really just depends on your values and what you want from life.

If you were 80 years old, looking back on your life, what would you have wished that you'd done with it? Take a moment to think about what you care about and what living a successful life means to you.

LOOKOUT!

Sometimes clients will say to me, "I don't care about the money." What they often express is a need for nourishment from other elements of a job—such as the lifestyle or environment. It's perfectly fine to have this attitude, but take caution. Even if having a lavish lifestyle isn't one of your values, it's still important to pay attention to your financial health and sense of balance.

I often think of a story I read about a financial advisor who said his dad always had a laissez faire attitude about money, claiming to be above caring about it. In his old age, this father wound up moving in with a friend because he didn't have enough to support himself. The son asked his father, "Who do you think thinks about money more now—you or Bill Gates?" In response, the father said, "Oh, me, for sure." Ignoring our finances, particularly how we will care for ourselves after our prime working years, is not a wise strategy. In fact, it's devoid of strategy.

That said, there are many spectrums of financial well-being, and the level of financial success and security you aspire to is an intensely personal choice.

For example, one author of a popular science fiction series offered the following piece of advice to aspiring writers: "Learn to live cheaply." It took this author twelve years to get to the point where one of his books reached mainstream success—so he had to figure out how to make ends meet while he cultivated his skill at storytelling. His strategy was uncomplicated. He lowered his expenses during those initial years of his career as a way of coping with his minimal income. As a result, he lived a more modest life. That choice and trade-off paid off in this particular author's case, as it gave him time to develop his craft.

I heard a similar story from a small business owner who mentioned to an audience that she went through a period where she made a choice to live in her office for a year to save money during her first year in business. She knew what she wanted to do, got creative with her living arrangement, and pulled it off.

I'll note that single individuals have more freedom to make extreme financial decisions like these than heads of families. An audience member who heard the small business woman's story said to me afterwards, "That's all well and good, but what if you have other mouths to feed?" Her point is well-taken, and true. You want to be responsible and thoughtful about how your decisions impact those living under your financial care. That responsibility is part of your life's work, and will, and should, impact any person's range of choices.

I think the trick is to be thoughtful about the implications of your financial choices, while also being careful not to use your responsibilities as an excuse to hide from the life you're really wanting. It's a fine line to walk and often involves coming up with a solution like Tom did, to transition with a short term plan (staying in his current job and saving) and a long term plan (moving on to more fulfilling work to boost his quality of life).

EXERCISES

FINANCIAL TOLL EXERCISE

What is the cost of your paycheck? Consider how your job or career path currently impacts the following areas of your life:

Health

_____

_____

State of Mind

_____

_____

Family

_____

_____

Community

_____

_____

Hobbies

_____

_____

Downtime

_____

_____

Friendships

_____

_____

Spirituality

_____

_____

WHAT'S YOUR PERSONAL DEFINITION OF CAREER SUCCESS?

Prestige and money often go hand in hand. However, a lucrative, socially-acceptable career achievement is not the gold standard of success. Success is contingent on individual desires and priorities and means matching up your life with what you want. It's OK to be whatever level of achiever you are. It can take a bit of courage to share who you are and what you want, but it really is OK to be yourself. Getting in touch with who you are is a form of success in and of itself!

Take a moment to define your personal definition of career and life success. Write it below and on the next page.

_____

_____

_____

_____

_____

_____

_____

_____

GET THE FINANCIAL FACTS

Let's be honest. In many cases, making a career change is going to result in a reduction in salary (at least temporarily). When we undergo any transitions in life, there are logistical snags and things to get used to. When it comes to making big shifts in our professional lives, it's only natural that some recalibration would need to happen as well.

But don't fear! We simply need to look this fact in the eye and get clarity on what this could mean rather than having it linger in the background as a frightening unknown.

Sit down with your finances and figure out just how low you could go salary or income-wise. (Remember to take taxes, insurance, rainy day funds, and retirement savings into account.)

Investigate your priorities and try to get curious rather than preemptively stressed out about the things you'll need to sacrifice. What would you be willing to cut or down-grade in order to make a lower salary work? What could you swing for a temporary period as you gain a foothold in a new career path?

By no means am I saying you should aim for a low salary. But I do want you to get clear on what your family's financial boundaries are so that you can respect them as you make a plan for moving forward.

Include your financial facts below.

Current Expenses

_____

Minimum Living Expenses

_____

Savings

_____

Number of Months of Cushion

_____

Minimum Required Monthly Earnings

_____

COACH'S NOTE

There are three "selves" we can be taking care of as adults (in addition to our responsibilities to others).

1) **The first self is the "in the moment" self.**
   Taking care of the "in the moment" self means tending to our immediate physical, mental, and emotional needs. Most advertisements are aimed at this self, as

immediacy sells: how can you feel better and be happier right *now*? Spending time doing activities you enjoy or being a part of environments that feel natural are methods of caring for this self, as are being mindful and practicing gratitude.

2) **The second self is the "just in case" self.**
   Tending to the "just in case" self means building up reserves in case something goes wrong. These could be monetary, relational, or resilience reserves. Building up a rainy day fund and having health insurance are examples of caring for this self.

3) **The third self is our "future" self.**
   Even if we love our work in the present, it's a kindness to our older, "future" self to plan for a time when we won't be working. Finance gurus (and many parents) hit this future planning area hard. Saving for retirement is a prime example of caring for this self. Creating healthy habits for yourself today is another example of caring for your tomorrow.

Consider three very broad categories that span each of these selves: your money, your well-being, and your relationships. Imagine a 3×3 chart. Which "self" are you the best at taking care of? Which area are you putting most of your focus towards? What "selves" or areas are you neglecting?

There are certainly times where it's appropriate to forego a "self" or an area temporarily. For example, I did not save for retirement for a few of the early years of my business. While this isn't financially ideal for "future" self, making that sacrifice is part of what helped me through leaner times. There's also a consequence to this neglect. It means I need to be more aggressive about caring for "future" self for the rest of my working years to catch up.

There are also instances where people neglect the "in the moment" self to push through a busy period or reach a goal. Again, this is not the end of the world. After a short-term push, you may want to give your "in the moment" self some TLC. For a really extended push, there could be consequences to your well-being and relationships that would require even more attention down the road.

My goal with this framework is to help you become more aware of quality of life as something to prioritize. It's easy to get sucked into a particular lifestyle and forget about all of the different ways we can be taking good care of ourselves.

CAREER MYTH: YOUR CAREER CAN KEEP YOU SAFE

We all have a core desire to keep ourselves and those we love safe and secure. We yearn for consistency. Stability. A sense of guarantee. We'd like to avoid suffering the pain of injury or loss. We want to know that everything's going to be alright.

Career choices are not immune to this drive. In fact, a large element of our careers is the level of security they provide.

Some industries are evergreen, with consistently solid job prospects. Other types of work face boom and bust cycles. Then there's the type of employment you pursue—full-time employee, contractor, freelance worker, or entrepreneur. Each type of employment has a varying level of stability.

Some of us may consciously choose a career path because of the element of security it provides. Others may neglect to consider the security factor at all and only later recognize the repercussions of their choices.

There are two contradictory truths that I know for sure when it comes to the subject of security and career choices.

The first is that no career path can provide you with security. No job is ever guaranteed. A steady paycheck will not ward off all of life's potential calamities. Plus, it's possible to feel insecure anywhere, even in an ostensibly "secure" job.

The second is that our careers can provide us with security. They can be the means by which we store up reserves in case of a rainy day. Similarly, they can give us health insurance and retirement plans. On another level, careers can be thought of as a place for us to grow into more confident and capable versions of ourselves, increasing our self-assurance.

Sometimes in our dogged pursuit of security and staying safe we can forget that this is life—that it is meant to be lived and that there are no guarantees. We perceive danger that may be nothing more than our own imagination. We forget that the sky will not fall when we step away from our familiar lifestyle and comforts.

And sometimes in our fervent desire for freedom or passion, we neglect the kindness of taking care of ourselves financially. We might feel frightened about losing control or settling. But we begin to yearn for more predictability and for greater financial freedom.

Each of us is dancing with an element of security in our careers. Is your current level of security too small, too large, or just right? The trick is to find a level that works for you.

While the past three chapters have focused on our internal dialogue and desires, there is also always an external dialogue going on in our heads about our career choices. What will people think!? Learn how to deal with the influence of other's opinions in the next chapter.

Chapter 7

ACKNOWLEDGING WHAT
YOU REALLY WANT

---

*At each and every moment in life, we are
swimming in the water of other people's opinions.
Regardless of whether you're a social butterfly,
have a smaller social circle, or tend to keep to
yourself, there are inevitably people in your life
such as family, teachers, mentors, friends, and
even celebrities who influence your thoughts and
behaviors. This can be a positive force in our lives,
as those around us often provide valuable advice
and support. However, when it comes to figuring
out big transitions in our lives (such as a career
change), the opinions, judgments and expectations
of others can be detrimentally influential—
especially if we let them go unchecked. Read
Jaime's story to learn how to tune into your social
environment more sensitively in order to harness it
to your advantage.*

Jaime reached out to me after having spent two decades
working in IT. He was consistently regarded as successful by
supervisors in the different positions he held and was often

promoted into roles with greater responsibility. He currently worked at the Vice President level for a well-known company headquartered in Hartford, Connecticut. His esteemed title was all the more noteworthy to me because Jaime did not have much enthusiasm for his work—at all. In fact, he didn't even feel that his main daily tasks played to his strengths. Jaime's work ethic and easygoing personality had carried him quite far.

"I have no idea what I want to be doing," Jaime told me, "But I just know that this isn't it."

Jaime told me repeatedly that he was completely at a loss for what kind of work he'd prefer to be doing—but I suspected differently. He demonstrated a clear sense of what his strengths and interests were in my initial questionnaire, so I suspected something else was going on.

His responses to the questionnaire all pointed to a strong interest in pursuing work where he would be helping others in some capacity. He'd noted mentoring as one of his favorite responsibilities in his current role. Jaime had also been participating in a leadership course in his spare time, simply because he was interested in improving his managerial skills. It was clear that fostering interpersonal relationships was a key priority for Jaime in his professional life. He told me in passing that he often read blogs about recent research in psychology.

So, during our first session, I asked Jaime about this clear thread that I had noticed. "You seem to have a strong leaning toward people stuff and helping others. Have you ever thought about working in a helping profession?" I asked.

"It's interesting that you say that," Jaime began, "I never thought of myself as being all that skilled with people. But the older I get, the more I realize I have a knack for understanding where others are coming from. I'm a good listener, and I enjoy being there for people."

I was not surprised by Jaime's response given what I'd observed. But I wanted to invite us to explore his interests further. "I'm curious as to whether or not you've ever mentioned your interest in potentially working in a helping profession to anyone," I asked Jaime.

"I didn't have to. My mom's sister spent a long time working with a therapist, and everyone in my family knows it didn't help her," Jaime explained. "There's a lot of judgment around helping professions in my family. They think that anyone who needs to get help isn't strong. I've thought about being a counselor or a coach, but I never mentioned it to anyone in my family. I'm pretty sure I know what they'd say," Jaime admitted with a little laugh.

"Sure," I said.

"I just worry about what everyone will think if I switch to a helping profession from the IT work I'm currently doing. My family really respects the tech world. They'll probably judge me and look down on my choices. I can't seem to move forward," Jaime continued.

There are plenty of hurdles involved in transitioning from IT to a helping profession, but in Jaime's case the biggest hurdle was his social environment. His fear of judgments from those around him was primarily what was blocking him from making any forward progress. On some level, he'd internalized the opinions of those around him, and he didn't think it was OK to want what he really wanted. So after mentally crossing off the possibility of working in a helping profession, Jaime was unable to get in touch with other career possibilities that interested him. By over-emphasizing the opinions of others, Jaime had obscured his own opinions, which is why he told me that he didn't know what he wanted.

The interesting thing about Jaime's case was that the people he was most concerned about impressing were an incredibly small selection of people: his nuclear family. His family members were the people with whom he interacted most regularly, so they comprised an essential core of his social world. However, Jaime was overlooking the obvious fact that his family's judgments were not a representative selection of all possible opinions about his choices. They were a tiny population, who happened to hold one belief. There are many other people who hold the belief that people who work in helping professions are wonderful. Jaime just hadn't been exposed to those perspectives, so he wasn't aware of them.

Jaime and I worked together in my Career Direction Clarity + Action Plan career coaching program. In our work together, Jaime and I primarily focused on helping him release the opinions of those around him. He had been dealing with a self-created obstacle: internalizing the judgments of others as fact. He was ready to empower himself with a new perspective, and was interested in increasing his level of Fulfillment in his work as a result.

We started off with a Body Compass exercise, a technique I learned from Martha Beck.

The central idea behind the Body Compass exercise is that we have a physical response to things that attract or repel our essential self. Our minds may feel convoluted and confused about what we're wanting, but our bodies tell a much simpler tale.

I explained this concept to Jaime, and walked him through the exercise. "We're going to help orient you to your physical reaction to both a negative and positive memory," I said. "From there, we'll create a scale from which you can test your reaction to other ideas. This will help you to clarify what you're truly wanting and assist you in recognizing the difference between your desires and your social environment's desires."

I had Jaime close his eyes and recall a particularly negative memory, bringing it fully to life with all his senses. Then I asked him to describe the physical sensations the memory brought up. I wasn't interested in details of the memory itself, but rather what he felt physically in response to the memory.

"I felt my chest tighten up right away. It feels like a weight is pushing down on me. My forehead is furrowed. I feel heavy all over," Jaime described to me.

"Great, now if you had to name this physical sensation using any language you wanted, what would it be?" I asked.

"Black sea," Jaime answered, after just a moment's thought.

"OK, and if you were to give this 'black sea' sensation a number on a scale of -10 to +10, where would you rank it? Negative 10 would rate as awful and positive 10 would rate as wonderful."

"It's pretty low. I'd give it a negative seven," Jaime told me.

"Alright, now we're going to do the same process, but this time with a positive memory. Shake out your body a little bit. And now think of a particularly positive time in your life. You might have been with people you loved, doing something you really enjoyed, or in a favorite place. Again, bring this memory into your mind's eye and just notice how you respond to the memory in your body."

"The first thing I notice is that my shoulders are relaxing a bit. I feel them settling back, and I'm sitting up straighter. There's a slight smile on my face. My arms and legs feel activated, like they're ready to go."

"Perfect. Now if you were to name this physical sensation,

what would it be?"

"Let's see . . . It's a peaceful, fluid feeling."

"Ok. So what number would you give the 'peaceful, fluid feeling' on a scale of -10 to +10?"

"It'd be a positive eight."

"Great. Now we have a baseline scale of what a negative experience and a positive experience feel like for you in your body. Again, shake out your body a little bit. Now imagine working in IT for the next several years and notice how you physically respond."

I heard Jaime take in a big intake of breath.

"Oh, right away I feel that heaviness. It's surprisingly strong. I'd say it's about a negative six."

"Lovely. You might see what's coming next," I joked, introducing the next step. "Now shake out your body and imagine working in a helping profession for the next several years."

"Wow. It's not all the way up to the peaceful, fluid feeling, but similarly, my whole body lifted and felt much lighter."

As Jaime and I continued working together, we regularly referred to the information that he had gleaned during the Body Compass exercise. Any time he felt confused about what he wanted, we'd refer to the scale he came up with. Having these reference points helped him to re-center and trust that he was on the right path for him, especially since they were tethered to his individual experience.

We also spent time identifying the specific people he was most concerned about impressing in his life. It turned out to be just three people: his parents and a respected colleague at work. I explained that his social environment would always influence him, and that he shouldn't feel bad about this very normal dynamic. But what Jaime had not realized was that he could seek out supportive social influencers to balance the opinions of his parents and this particular colleague. While his parents would always be his parents and would always play an important role in his life, he realized that he could think more thoughtfully about expanding his social circle to include alternative mentoring figures that might be more accepting of the career he truly wanted to pursue.

By working with me, someone who thought highly of helping professions, Jaime had already started to build an increased sense of social support for the career path he wanted to explore. And with my encouragement, he quickly made connections at a local counseling organization, where he ended up meeting several other supportive individuals. Suddenly, he not only had a small network of friends who would give him social approval and support, but he also had people who could provide him with useful information about potential career paths.

CORE CONCEPT

According to sociologist and life coach Martha Beck, we all have two "selves" who influence our decisions about the direction of our lives. These selves are known as the social self and the essential self.

The social self is motivated by external pressures—what people around us will think of our decisions. The social self is the part of you who bites your tongue when your boss asks you to stay late yet again. You want to say something to assert your boundaries, but you don't because your social self feels pressured, and believes that being deferential will help you keep your job.

The social self helps us to fit in with those around us. Its primary goal is to please others. In fact, our social selves would love for us to do anything to affirm that we are liked, respected, and admired. The social self desperately wants to avoid being looked down upon or scrutinized by others. In response to any impulses you have, the social self constantly cautions, "But what will other people think?!"

The value system upheld by the social self is influenced by the specific values of the unique social systems to which each of us belongs. The son of a gardener and a goldsmith in California will likely have a different set of social directives than the daughter of a lawyer and an accountant in Texas. Values differ based on family history, geographic location, profession, socioeconomic status, and a whole host of other factors.

In contrast to the social self, there's the essential self. This is our essence—who we really are. The essential self embodies all of our authentic preferences, likes, and dislikes. The essential self is something that is with us from birth, and it is immutable. The essential self does not change based on the culture in which we live. We would love the same certain things more than others whether we were born in Wyoming, Australia, or the Czech Republic.

The essential self is motivated by internal preferences. The essential self of an engineer could be expressed by spending all day creating a cool computer program, because that activity is something that person loves to do.

When the drives of the social self and the essential self are in conflict, many people disconnect from what they truly want to do (the desires of the essential self) in order to be who they think they should be (the desires of the social self).

When we listen to the wisdom and preferences of the essential self, we live more fulfilling lives. When you add things into your life that you intrinsically enjoy and take out things that you intrinsically dislike, you wind up liking your life a lot more.

This sounds simple on the surface, but simplicity doesn't always make things easy. For many people, tapping into the essential self presents an enigma. Often, the essential self has been buried due to years of conforming to the expectations of other people in our lives and of society.

LOOKOUT!

My client, Lucy, was struggling to make progress. Every session we had together started with Lucy sharing confusion and doubt about what she wanted to do with her life. And it ended with her feeling more connected to what she actually wanted. Lucy wanted to become a teacher because she loved working with kids and wanted to make a difference in their lives.

I knew from my discussions with Lucy that she was particularly close to her father. I also knew that her father had a strong personal agenda about what career she should pursue. Her father wanted her to become an actuary because he knew it would be a stable and lucrative career path for her.

Lucy and I went in circles for a few weeks before I realized what was happening. During our sessions, I always felt the beginnings of progress. Lucy would begin to open up to me, and I would ask questions to help her connect with a career path that she most wanted. But her sense of clarity and motivation never seemed to accelerate. I was confused until I realized that between our sessions, Lucy was having intense conversations with her father about her possible career path as a teacher. The strength of his opinions put her back in a confused state every time she spoke to him.

If you have a person in your social circle who has a strong voice and set of opinions about your life choices, please be careful about using them as a confidante while you are contemplating a career change. Their influence, particularly if it's negative, can keep you stuck, just as Lucy experienced.

Of course, it makes sense to talk over decisions with loved ones. But particularly at very early stages in a career change process, your priority should be to protect the dream you are exploring. Give yourself time and space in a safe environment to develop your confidence in what you're wanting before sharing it with the world.

If you don't have a supportive social environment, be sure to sign up for the Step-By-Step Career Change E-Course for free at www.cardycareercoaching.com/bookgift. I'll provide you with weekly encouragement and support to move forward and make progress. Or consider working with me through one of my three signature career coaching programs. Sometimes having one person in your corner can make all the difference, and I'd be happy to be in yours.

EXERCISES

BODY COMPASS

Our bodies are connected to our essential self. Our brains are connected to our social self. In this way, our bodies have more wisdom about our truest path than our minds. Our bodies respond with strength to truth and with weakness to lies. We can use the physical reactions our bodies provide to different scenarios as a compass for whether we are on the right track or not.

This exercise will help you to identify and name the physical sensations associated with the essential self saying yes and no.

You will run through two scenarios: one negative and one positive.

First, think of a particularly negative experience in your life. You may have been around people that you didn't like or doing an activity that you hated. Bring this memory as fully into your brain as possible. Integrate all five senses into the memory. Re-connect with the smells, sounds, sights, tactile sensations, and tastes associated with the memory. Keep the memory in your mind as you scan your body from your feet to your head. Notice how your body feels in the present moment. Write down your physical reactions to this memory.

My body responds to my essential self saying no by:

_____

_____

_____

Now create a trigger phrase for this physical feeling. If you were to create a metaphor for this feeling what would it be? What color would it be?

_____

_____

_____

_____

Trigger phrase:

_____

_____

If you could rate this feeling on a scale of -10 to 0, where would you place it?

_____

Shake your body out. Repeat the above instructions, this time with a positive memory. My body responds to my essential self saying yes by:

_____

_____

Trigger phrase:

_____

_____

If you could rate this feeling on a scale of 0 to +10, where would you place it?

_____

Test how your body responds to a couple of different career possibilities by imagining those scenarios and noticing your body's reaction. (You could try your current job along with other career ideas you've considered.) How would you rate your response on a scale of -10 to +10?

_____

_____

_____

_____

NAME YOUR EVERYBODY

This exercise is based on concepts presented in Martha Beck's *Finding Your Own North Star*. Mentally walk through your immediate social environment. As you go through each person, note whether they are generally negative, neutral, or supportive about career ideas you've mentioned. Also, note if they have a strong opinion or agenda regarding what they think that you ought to be doing with your life. Remember to be careful about who you share this career exploration process with. Supportive people are the ideal choices.

	Negative, Neutral, or Supportive?	Agenda?
Family		
Friends		

Coworkers		
Groups		
Others		

COACH'S NOTE

When considering a career path, remember that you have the most insight into what you want, who you might become, and where you thrive. Others in your life can only guess at what could be a potentially rewarding career path for you. They may provide career guidance based on what they perceive to be the "best" jobs of the day, which may involve things that are completely unrelated to who you are or what you want. There are three things to consider about the opinions of those around you.

1) Family members may not see you as separate from themselves and may project their career aspirations or latent dreams onto you. Trust your internal sense of yourself, and be aware of the times you feel yourself internalizing family members' opinions and judgments.

This is easy to do, and a normal reaction—so just try to notice it. You may feel a bit vague about exactly what you want to be doing, but in all likelihood you have a sense of career paths that feel "off" when they are presented to you. It will take work and effort to realize a career path to which you feel deeply connected, and oftentimes people in your life may not see your vision until after you've put in the work to show them what you can do. That's OK. You don't need to convince everyone in your social environment at the onset of your pursuit of a particular path. You just need to convince yourself and make sure you're getting enough social support from other people to keep yourself going.

2) Keep in mind that, in general, most people don't care that much about any decision you make, career-wise or otherwise. This sounds cold—but it's actually a huge relief. Additionally, most people's opinions are fickle. Someone may initially judge you for a choice you make. But say that same person sees how well you are doing after your transition into a new field. That person will likely will change their mind and get on board with your decision—after you've made it.

3) Also know that loved ones often want to protect those they care about from any sort of pain or disappointment. Know that there will be some of these emotions involved in most any career change, and they will be temporary. Pain and challenge are the forces that help us grow. By attempting to protect you from these experiences, loved ones may inadvertently be signing you up for the more persistent pain of lack of confidence or regret.

I often think of social expectations as the currents that run through our lives. If you aren't paying attention, those currents will direct your life. The trick is to lift your head up, pick a point on the horizon, hoist your sails, and start consciously moving in the direction you want.

CAREER MYTH: YOU CAN GO IT ALONE

While there may be people in your life who are not as supportive of your career aspirations as you'd like, there is also a greatly reduced chance of success when you try to go about any big life change alone. We need other people to connect us to opportunities, give us new information, and offer emotional support.

Follow these five steps to build support for your career change.

SHARE SELECTIVELY

In the early stages of a new career idea you want to be extra judicious about whom you share your dreams with.

Do you know someone who is generally positive, optimistic, and supportive? Someone who lives in the world of possibilities and gets excited by new ideas? That person is an encourager. And they are the people you want to be discussing your plans with when your ideas are new and tender. An encourager's presence alone has the potential to fan your tiny spark of an idea into a strong, steady flame.

Note that encouragers are often found *outside* of your immediate family. After all, the people who are closest to you are the ones who will be the most affected by your potential career change. The individuals who see you most regularly will likely be more resistant to your idea, simply because we all have a tendency to resist change.

Be particularly careful of sharing your ideas with people who both have a discouraging tendency and hold a big place in your psyche (e.g. parents or revered professors). Nothing will stop you short faster than their disapproval.

LET GO OF CONVINCING EVERYONE TO GET ON BOARD WITH YOUR PLANS

People often wait for permission from authority figures before going after their dream careers. Or they only want to do it if they know that their loved ones will be 100% supportive.

If someone in your life isn't behind your new career idea, they probably aren't going to change their mind anytime soon.

Avoid wasting your breath trying to convince them that your idea is fantastic, and don't make your choice to go after your dream conditional on someone else's approval. Doing this puts you in a powerless position and prevents you from actually trying your idea out in the real world.

Instead, try to accept that this is how your loved one feels at the moment, and put your energy toward building your support network through other, more viable avenues.

WORK WITH A COACH

Good career coaches are not only supportive and encouraging, but also have a multitude of psychological frameworks and techniques to help you stay on track with your career goals.

A casual acquaintance who provides encouragement can make a difference, but a structured coaching relationship can really take your career development efforts to the next level.

Since a coach is an objective third party, they will not have the same type of agenda or preconceived notion of you that a close relation might have.

Make sure to find a coach you respect, trust, and feel comfortable with. And don't hesitate to look around for a coach who will be an excellent fit for your specific situation.

SEEK OUT GROUPS OF PEOPLE LIKE YOU

While your career path could seem unconventional, there are undoubtedly other people who are already gainfully employed in your chosen field. There are also people who are aspiring to make it, just like you.

By finding groups of people in your chosen industry, you will expand your network and learn useful information; plus, you'll increase your sense social acceptance and feel more excitement and camaraderie around your professional interests.

When you join an organization, be especially diligent about connecting with groups and group members who strike you as successful—whether in terms of leadership, attitude, or work-life balance. Someone you admire will have the most to offer you and will help lift you up.

SURROUND YOURSELF WITH INSPIRATION

One final technique for strengthening your support system is to increase your connection to people whom you admire, but are unlikely to ever meet. These will be people (alive or deceased) whose lives and messages inspire you to be your best.

Create a collage of their faces and your favorite quotes. Look at it often, and use their wisdom and encouragement to your advantage.

Getting any career off the ground takes courage, patience, and persistence. It also takes people to encourage you when you're feeling down, connect you to helpful resources, and inspire you to strive for more.

Help your chances of success by taking one step to consciously build your support network today.

In the next chapter, we're going to focus on taking action. If you're like many of my clients, this may feel like an unwanted interruption to the mental work we've been doing thus far. But hang in there. Action is the critical piece of the puzzle that brings everything together. It's what makes transitions actually happen.

Chapter 8

TRANSITIONING FROM ANALYSIS TO ACTION

It can be extremely tempting to hang out in the safety of our own minds, even if our thought patterns are negative. After all, the familiar feels inherently safer, and keeps us from the trans-formational—but scary—step of having to "put ourselves out there" in order to bring about change in our lives. In this chapter, you'll read about Claire, a client who was stalling out because she was overly reliant on introspection. Read this chapter to get inspired to get out of your head and into the real world.

My client Claire reached out to me for help after attempting to sort out her career for many years on her own. She had worked her way up to a position as the office manager for a large medical practice in Boston, Massachusetts, but came home at the end of most days feeling both physically and emotionally drained, and generally unfulfilled by her daily work. When we began working together, Claire submitted one of the most thorough set of responses to my intake questions that I'd ever seen. She attached her Meyers Briggs results, her

DISC assessment, and a couple of pages of work on other exercises she'd completed that identified her core desired feelings and ideal work day.

I appreciated Claire's thoroughness and could tell that she was both totally miserable in her current job and totally determined to show up for our coaching sessions. I had no doubt that she wanted to get the most out of our time together.

I also recognized that despite the years that Claire had been stuck, she was mostly stuck due to utilizing an ineffective career transition methodology. Claire worked with me through my Just Get Me Pointed in the Right Direction program because she didn't need much more than directions on what she needed to do differently to actually make progress on her career issue.

During our first session, Claire and I identified the broad strokes of what she was looking for in her next career move. As you may have guessed, Claire enjoyed the process of investigation and research. She loved digging up information and finding answers to questions. She was passionate and organized, and loved to compile her findings as a means to find potential solutions to problems. She was methodical and persistent in her approach to work. She also happened to be fascinated by the topic of environmental conservation. She found she was naturally drawn to researching the ways in which individuals, businesses, and governments could reduce their environmental impact. I knew that she was looking to increase her level of Fulfillment from her job, and I kept all of this insight about Claire in mind during our work together.

To me, the field of environmental research was a clear guidepost for where Claire should start her process of exploration. But when I mentioned the idea of talking to people and testing out her hypothetical career path, Claire immediately pushed back.

"Isn't there an exercise or two you could give me to help me really narrow in on what I'm looking for?" Claire politely asked me. "I still feel pretty vague about what it is I want to do with my career."

"I understand that you are not at the point of 100% clarity regarding what you want to do next, and I know that completing exercises can feel productive, but we need to get you out of your head and into the world," I explained to Claire patiently. I wanted her to know both that her introspective work thus far was a great start, but also that she needed to start learning new things through experimentation. Introspection provides us with a starting place of where to look in life, but actually taking real world action is what allows us to find it.

I wanted to probe further to see whether or not she felt greater clarity from all of her self-reflection. "How many aptitude or personality tests have you taken?" I asked.

"I think about seven," she replied with a rueful laugh.

"And how much clearer are you feeling after taking those tests?" I prodded further.

"Not a whole lot," she said. "I'm still pretty muddled."

"I want to recognize that you've been putting a lot of effort into trying to figure this out," I commended her. "But now you need to take that effort and channel it into more productive behavior. It's going to feel less comfortable to talk to people who are doing environmental research than it did to sign up for a test, but you will make much more headway as a result."

Many people fall into the career crossroads trap that Claire was experiencing. They think that by reflecting long and hard enough (and in just the right way), they'll find their perfect career answer. When they are unsuccessful at uncovering a "light bulb moment," they assume the problem is with the particular test or reflection they attempted, so they continue spinning their wheels looking for a different assessment that will give them an answer. Little do they know that it is this behavior that is keeping them stuck in the same place.

Based on experience, I've realized that the issue underlying most cases like these is that individuals are using the wrong methodology altogether. Some introspection is helpful, sure. But too much thinking can become detrimental. When it comes to career changes, one's internal knowledge of different possibilities pales in comparison to the rich, vast universe of job realities.

There are so many jobs in the world that fall outside of the professions most of us learn about in elementary school—doctor, lawyer, teacher, accountant, engineer, and fire fighter. There are tons of opportunities that exist just outside of your cubicle, which means you probably don't even know that they exist yet. I know this to be true because not only have I peeked into the lives of clients who have worked as wildlife forensic specialists and greeting card writers (yes, both jobs actually exist!), but I've also spoken to over fifty distinct professional organizations. I know that to successfully home in on the career path you want, you'll need to interact with the real world by talking to people and being open to engaging with new experiences.

Let me put it this way: if you were about to move to a different country, one you'd never been to before and had no concrete knowledge about, it would make sense to begin by thinking about the type of area you'd like to live in. You could consider what you liked or didn't like about your current living situation. You could reflect on whether you wanted an urban, suburban, or rural area. You could make a list of the characteristics that would be most important to you in your new home.

But after a point, reflection would become useless! After all, your speculation about what it's like to live in a foreign country is speculative. In other words, thinking alone limits your perspective and results in a viewpoint that is likely riddled with assumptions.

To find your ideal location in this new country, you'd eventually need to learn more about it through reading, having conversations, or even "on the ground" investigation. You might talk to people who had lived there, read books and articles, or take a trip to scout out the lay of the land. After doing these things, you'd be much more prepared to make a better decision about where to settle down. And after a year of living in this new place, you'd be able to refine your idea of where you'd most want to be living even further.

Just as your ideal neighborhood in a new place is found by external exploration, your ideal career is similarly an exercise in exploring and trying different things out. Neither solution lies totally within you, but for many of us it's all too easy to slip into the cyclical mode of over-analyzing

Claire took my advice. Together, we identified a couple people with whom she could connect and some organizations for her to explore—both of which would hopefully help her to gain a better understanding of the environmental research field. At times, Claire was quite nervous to take (even small) steps in a new direction, but she bravely pushed through her discomfort.

During the more interactive and experiential part of Claire's career exploration process, she learned much more about the day-to-day of working in environmental research and the different job possibilities that were in the field. We talked through everything that she'd been learning, and Claire ultimately came to the conclusion that she wanted to become an Environmental Programs Analyst, a position that she had never even heard of before conducting her career exploration!

Could you use reminders about the real world actions you ought to be taking to get unstuck and on with your career? Sign up for my complimentary Step-By-Step Career Change E-Course at www.cardycareercoaching.com/bookgift for weekly, doable steps that will support you in gaining momentum with your career. I'll encourage you to be brave and cheer you on throughout your process.

CORE CONCEPTS

EARLY DISMISSAL

Early dismissal begins with a career idea. For example, "I'd love to be a veterinarian." You get excited about the idea for a short amount of time—an hour, a day, a week. *What fun to work with animals!* You think to yourself, ecstatic. *How great to be on my feet and working with people during the work day, instead of sitting in a cubicle.* You're enthralled.

But then, in the midst of dreaming about how wonderful it would be to this job, doubts begin to creep in. You start to think about specific challenges relating to your dream career path. You might think, "Oh, but vet school is so hard to get into." Or, "There are too many other people who want to be veterinarians." You begin feeling scared that this career might not work out for you. You mentally cross this idea off your potential careers list.

Note what is happening here. You've dismissed your career

idea out of hand in your mind before taking any external action toward it. You are mentally limiting yourself with self-created thought barriers and fears.

Often people who engage in early dismissal believe that they have no idea what career they would like to pursue. This is because they've dismissed the careers that they would actually find rewarding. Then they look around at the remaining career opportunities. None of them look all that great.

Combat early dismissal by giving yourself permission to explore career paths that are interesting to you, even if they initially feel totally impossible. Remember that exploration is like touring a new apartment or house. Just because you take a look doesn't mean that you have to move in. So take the pressure off, and remember that sometimes we scare ourselves by prematurely investing in a given situation! Explore. Investigate. Get curious.

INFORMATIONAL INTERVIEWS

An informational interview is an effort to learn more about a particular industry or career path by talking to someone who is currently working in that field. My clients often use this tool when they are exploring different career possibilities, as it helps them get a more concrete and detailed idea of what a particular job actually entails.

Informational interviews can also be utilized as a way to build connections during a job search. While informational interviews can lead to jobs, they are not the same as a job interview. Your overall approach ought to be one of curiosity and investigation. An informational interview is *not* the appropriate time to talk about why you are amazing and perfect for a certain job.

TEST EXPERIENCES

Test experiences are like test drives—you try out the actions that you think you would like to be doing for a career in a test environment. For example, a person who is interested in becoming a lawyer might participate in a mock trial program. Someone who is thinking of becoming a teacher might get involved in an afterschool mentoring program.

Often, our minds hold us back in this regard, thinking that we need to jump through a ton of hoops before we can experience a potential career path. We think we need to go back to school, start at the bottom of a new job hierarchy, or pay money to learn our trade. This can make exploring a new career path unnecessarily daunting. Trying to make a big investment for an outcome that is largely unknown is uncomfortable and can lead to a whole lot of stagnation.

Test experiences, on the other hand, are low investment and low commitment, and they have two huge benefits.

First, they provide you with a great deal of information about your desired career path. You may learn more about the day-to-day minutiae of the job, such as the unexpected challenges, or the kinds of people who are in the field. You'll also get to see how your essential self reacts to the proposed environment. You may get exposure to a related career that you hadn't heard of or thought about before. Or you may meet a new contact or reference that serves you down the road.

Second, taking small movements is the antidote to feeling stuck. It feels good to know that you are taking constructive action toward a better future. By making small moves in the form of test experiences, you show yourself that you're beginning to build momentum toward larger moves and larger decisions.

LOOKOUT!

In addition to getting lost in introspection, there are three other types of ineffective action that frequently keep people stuck.

One of the most common forms of wasted effort I see is misguided job searching. I am referring to those who put lots of time into online job searching before determining a targeted career path.

It's all too easy to sit behind a computer and send application after application out through online job search portals. The action is well-intentioned and may initially feel very productive, but it tends to be ultimately unproductive. Without thoughtful execution, premature job searching is a waste of time and energy, as it can lead to dead-ends and then further frustration and disappointment as a result. Take the time and energy to engage in a more deliberate and mindful process of career exploration. Get clearer about what you're looking for, while remembering that it's unlikely that you'll ever reach 100% clarity. Sure, conducting a career exploration will take a bit more effort than clicking "send" on an arbitrary job application. But it will it make your eventual job search much more effective.

The second most common way I see people taking unproductive action is staying within their comfort zone during career exploration. For example, informational interviewing is meant to stretch you into unfamiliar territory—to put you in touch with people with whom you might not otherwise interact. If you find yourself reaching out to people who are already in your network or who work at a job that is very similar to your current one, then you are probably wasting your time (unless you want to stay in the same field).

One of my clients conducted a slew of informational interviews before working with me, but still felt stuck. The tactic itself was not wrong, but she was interviewing people in her exact field—a field that she wanted to leave! Once she began venturing outside of this realm of comfort, the action became much more helpful and clarified what it was she really wanted to be doing.

The final type of unproductive action is premature dreaming. In the self-help world, I often notice an emphasis on imagination-focused exercises—such as making vision boards or a five-year end game, and connecting to desired feeling states. All of these are excellent tools, and yet I rarely use them with my clients, and have made that choice intentionally. Here's the thing: when you're making a career change, you're venturing into an unknown area. As a result, you won't have a complete grasp of the career path or lifestyle ramifications of your choice. Dreaming exercises are most productive when you have a real foothold in an area and want to improve it. This happens *after* you've made a change and have learned the landscape. In short, I want you to focus on taking productive action and cleaning up your mindset at this point in time. Save the dreaming for later, and you'll find you have a better chance of making those dreams come true.

EXERCISES

CAREER EXPLORATION EXERCISE

In this exercise, you'll look through a career database to identify jobs that seem appealing to you. A career database is a site that lists jobs and provides a brief summary of the associated work. At the time of this writing, I prefer the site www.insidejobs.com because it is searchable and has compelling visual elements. You can also search "career database" for other aggregate career listings online. While these sites contain a tremendous variety of jobs, they may miss newer fields or niched areas, so keep that in mind during your search.

Play with the different selections available on the Inside Jobs site homepage (such as "what do you like?" and "what are you good at?") to identify jobs that look appealing to you based on the themes listed above and your interests. Try using the search bar to focus your attention on more specific areas from the themes you uncovered in Chapter 2.

One way to do this that might be helpful is to imagine you have seven lives. With each life you can do something totally different. In this imaginary scenario, all jobs are paid the same and valued by society equally. What different jobs would pick in this scenario?

For now, I'd like you to approach this exercise without giving thought to practical concerns. Forget about trying to figure out the "how" of transitioning into the jobs you identify. Ignore the financial ramifications of what you're picking and the feasibility of attaining what you want. Your task is just to match up your interests with jobs that are in alignment with them.

Write down the jobs that appeal to you in the lines below. Once you've hit your limit on potential career paths (and it may take a little while—the site I recommended has a very extensive and sometimes repetitive listing system), put a star next to the careers that seem most interesting to you.

List your jobs here.

_____

_____

_____

_____

_____

_____

_____

MAKE A CAREER HYPOTHESIS

In most cases, I see people list a number of related jobs, along with a few one off outliers. Generally, the jobs that are represented a couple times indicate a stronger interest.

Review your list of interesting jobs and pick your favorite(s). Then narrow it down to one job. We will use this job as our initial career hypothesis. Fill it in below.

_____

_____

_____

_____

You'll start your career exploration with this career hypothesis. As you explore and learn more about the initial career path you've chosen, you'll get a better understanding of the job and the path to get there. Pay attention to your reactions to see if you are still enthusiastic about the field. If so, it will be time to move into making a transition plan for yourself. And if not, you can revise your hypothesis to something different.

INFORMATIONAL INTERVIEW BRAINSTORM

Who do I know who is currently working in the field I'm considering? List current connections here.

_____

_____

_____

_____

_____

Who could I ask to see if they know anyone working in the field I'm considering? (Think of friends, family, acquaintances, former colleagues, former classmates, professors, or people in volunteer or extracurricular activities in which you've been involved.) List your supporters here.

_____

_____

_____

_____

_____

Use LinkedIn to see who your connections are, and who their connections are. Try to see if there is anyone to whom you could ask for an introduction. List these people here.

_____

_____

_____

_____

_____

Utilize LinkedIn's alumni tool (http://blog.linkedin.com/2013/01/30/start-mapping-your-career-with-linkedin-alumni/) to find people who have gone to your high school, undergraduate, or graduate programs, and who are now working in the field you are considering (or a related field). The school commonality tends to cultivate warmer connections. Be sure to mention your alma mater when you reach out. List these potential connections here.

_____

_____

_____

_____

_____

Keep track of everyone you are connecting to on a spreadsheet that lists the name, date of your initial reach out, how you're connected, and the date you plan to follow-up. Realize that you will probably need to send a second, follow-up email if the person doesn't get back to you. I would recommend doing this about a week after the initial request.

Sample Questions

What does the day to day of your job entail?

What are your favorite parts of your job?

What are the things that annoy you about your job?

What surprised you about your job?

What advice would you have for someone who is considering this field?

What are the attributes of people who are successful at this job?

What qualifications are needed to get this job?

What education or trainings would you most recommend?

Are there any industry associations (groups) or publications that you would recommend?

What type of salary could I expect when I enter this industry?

What is the salary potential for this job?

The Magic Questions—be sure to ask one of these!!!

Ask for other connections. For example:

- Who else would you recommend I talk to?
- Do you know anyone else who I could talk to about X, Y, or Z?
- Would you mind introducing me to two other people in your field?

Keep in Mind

As you're conducting informational interviews, remember that you want to focus on whether or not the actual job that they're doing sounds appealing to you. You can check in with yourself using the Body Compass exercise, noticing how you physically respond to the conversation. Or, note how energized or depleted you feel after hearing about the job. This can be a powerful indicator of what your next course of action should be.

Ideally, we're looking for a job description that has you leaning forward in your chair, either metaphorically or literally. You may hit it with your first hypothesis, or we may need to revise a bit based on what you learn. Either way is fine. It's easy enough to change course at this exploratory stage of the game.

The Thank You

After conducting an informational interview, be sure to thank the person for their time. Note how much you appreciated their insight. Mention one or two comments that they made that you found particularly helpful. Wish them well.

The Update

This email is for when you followed someone's advice, and it worked. It's for when you have a follow-up question. It's for when you want to grease the wheels for a connection to a relevant job. The bottom line is that you want to keep the person with whom you spoke apprised of what's going on as it relates to your conversation. You wouldn't want to send one of these update emails every week, but every few months or so would be appropriate.

TEST EXPERIENCE BRAINSTORM OF YOUR CAREER HYPOTHESIS

Brainstorm 10 ways that you could move closer to your career hypothesis through a test experience.

When completing this exercise, try to move as close as possible to a 3-D experience of your desired career path. For example, if you are energized by the idea of being a veterinarian, a 3-D experience would involve actually interacting with live animals. You could also look for a professional organization or association for veterinarians and attend a meeting or conference.

10 Ways You Could Move Closer to the Actual Experience of Your Career Hypothesis*

_____

_____

_____

_____

_____

_____

_____

_____

_____

_____

*without going back to school, taking a full-time job, or paying an arm and a leg

Most Appealing Ideas:

_____

_____

_____

COACH'S NOTE

Reaching out for informational interviews can feel uncomfortable. But recognize that this discomfort is simply part of
the process. Expect it to be there and be willing to experience
a bit of nervousness, particularly if you are reaching out to a
cold connection (e.g. someone you don't know very well). A
willingness to go through discomfort and persistence are the
two qualities you'll most need to work through the informational interviewing process.

Keep in mind that people generally want to be helpful
to others and are often willing to take a bit of time to share
their story and advice. It's flattering to be asked for guidance
and fun to share a personal perspective. Also, people who
are successful in a particular career usually recognize that
they didn't get there all by themselves. They had help. As a
result, they may be eager to pay it forward and be of service to
others. That said, it's nothing personal if someone declines (or
ignores) your request or is unable to talk with you. Stick with
the process and ask someone else. Keep asking people until
you accomplish this task. It may take several attempts.

If you find yourself not taking the actions described in
this chapter (talking to people and getting out into the real
world in other ways), revisit the materials in Chapter 5 to see
if you can find a thought that isn't supporting you, along with

a better feeling perspective that will make it easier for you to move forward.

CAREER MYTH: THE HOBBY HOAX

A great place to start when you're thinking about your career direction is to consider the environments and activities that you naturally gravitate towards.

However, there's one particular way the question "what do I like?" can be wielded unproductively. I call this the hobby hoax.

The hobby hoax occurs when you have a passing interest in a particular topic. For example, you remember enjoying working through a book on calligraphy. Or you had a blast taking a tap dance class with a friend.

But should you move into a career in one of these "fun" areas? That's the big question. Here's a quick litmus test to see if the hobby you enjoyed in passing will hold water as a career.

When you think about doing that particular activity are you thinking about it solely from the perspective of improving your own skills? Like becoming a better mime? Or finally becoming fluent in Chinese?

You're probably on the wrong track if you're envisioning a lot of investment in learning and improving yourself instead of contributing to others.

I've seen people go into hobby professions successfully. (A hobby profession is one where there are a select group of people who make their living in that field, and there are also many people who enjoy participating in that activity in an amateur or hobby-like way. Athletics, arts, lifestyle, and languages are all examples of these fields.)

What differentiates people who work in a hobby profession from those who enjoy doing the activity on the weekend is the level of investment and enthusiasm. For those who work in a hobby profession, the particular hobby is the thing that they can't NOT do. And their skill level is such that when they do their work, they can be of benefit to others.

My point here is not to discourage you from going into a profession that relates to a hobby you enjoy. It's just to make a subtle distinction. Sometimes, considering a fleeting interest as a career possibility can actually take you down an unfruitful path.

Spending time in a classroom environment trying to improve your skills at a given hobby can actually be a way to hide from what you have to offer the world. Even if the process of developing a skill is arduous, it can still keep you squarely in your comfort zone. Step outside of this familiar area. Be willing to experience discomfort and rejection. Be bold, and show us what you've really got.

In this chapter, my focus has been to give you advice that will help you get out of your head and into the real world. Your willingness to take these small actions will impact your ability to improve your career. The next two chapters will provide you with further guidance about how to take action, what actions to take when, and why these steps can often be so challenging!

Chapter 9

MOVING THROUGH FEAR

If you're afraid of making a career change, you're not alone. The most important thing you'll glean from this chapter is that fear comes up for 100% of my clients when they consider a career change. It's not that my clients are scaredy-cats. It's that fear is a completely natural response to the unknown (which is what happens when we attempt to change our careers). Fear is a survival mechanism: our bodies literally pump out hormones like adrenaline and norepinephrine when we are faced with an unfamiliar situation, thought or feeling. So the first essential step is shifting your expectations: welcome fear as part of the process. In this chapter, you'll read how I guided my client Suzanna through her fears and into the possibilities that were waiting on the other side of them.

My pulse is racing and my breathing is shallower than usual. There's a major sensation in my chest, sort of like taking in a big inhale," my client Suzanna described to me nervously.

Suzanna was a new client in my Career Direction Clarity + Action Plan program, which provides more extensive support for clients dealing with obstacles, unhelpful thought patterns, fears, and concerns about what other people will think. She and I were sitting in a comfortable coffee shop in Arlington, Virginia with no visible threats around us. I had asked Suzanna to close her eyes and check in with how she physically felt when she imagined putting up her LinkedIn profile to support her in connecting with old classmates, friends, and colleagues. Her response was the description of a physical manifestation of fear.

Shortly after completing her Master's program as a developmental physical therapist, Suzanna had experienced two significant deaths in her family. Reeling from these losses, Suzanna found herself directing most of her energy towards her family. She shifted her priorities away from work and towards spending time with her older sister, who had been most affected by the family's losses.

These were deliberate choices, but they did come with consequences. Not only did she have to deal with grief, but Suzanna had also temporarily stepped out of the workforce, and felt disconnected from her career. She had reached out to me to help her reconnect with her professional identity. She was particularly interested in finding a greater sense of Fulfillment from work while also improving her Financial Health.

One of Suzanna's biggest obstacles was internal—a deep fear of rejection, which she attributed to insecurity about the gap in her resume.

Months before contacting me, Suzanna had been thinking about making a LinkedIn account, but there was something keeping her paralyzed—so she never pulled the trigger. Even when she *imagined* signing up for the site, as I had instructed her to do, she had a vivid and immediate feeling of fear.

I knew then that Suzanna and I were going to work together on dealing with her fear, and I had an exercise in mind. Before beginning it, I explained to Suzanna that the exercise involved *listening to*—rather than turning away from—her fears. When it comes to uncomfortable feelings like fear, anxiety, anger, and more, our typical inclination is to push away or ignore them in an effort to avoid the unpleasant sensations they bring up.

This is a normal reaction, but here's the thing: our fears have something to tell us. I explained this to Suzanna, and told her that we were going to cozy up with her fears and pay attention to them, much like the way a kind adult would care for a frightened child. I emphasized that even though physical sensations would come up, she was safe with me, and that I wasn't going to ask her to do anything she did not want to do. We were merely going to observe her fear.

I began the exercise by describing Suzanna's sensations of fear back to her: "So you said you're feeling on edge. Your pulse is racing, your breathing is shallow, and there's a feeling in your chest. If you were to use an image to describe this physical feeling, what would it be?" I asked Suzanna.

Suzanna took a deep breath.

"This is weird, but what's coming to mind is the image of a runner at the starting line of a men's track race. The stands are full, and everyone is watching," Suzanna explained.

"Great," I said. "Now I want you to focus on the runner. See him in your mind's eye and gently ask the runner what he needs. You may get a reply. You may not. Either way is OK," I explained.

Suzanna was quiet for a few moments.

"The runner needs to focus on his own actions and ignore

the crowd."

"Excellent. Is there anything else the runner needs?" I questioned.

"To get moving. I think the runner has been crouched in the starting position for so long that it's gotten really uncomfortable. If he were to actually start the race, he'd be focused on his own actions, rather than the perceptions of the crowd. Then he'd be less scared," Suzanna told me.

"Does the runner have anything else to say?" I checked.

"Nope, I think that's about it," Suzanna said.

"OK, great. Mentally thank the runner for chatting with you. Then open your eyes," I instructed. "How does the runner's message apply to the real world of you attempting to put up your LinkedIn profile?"

"That's pretty clear. What's making me scared is dawdling at the starting line, worrying too much about what other people will think of me. I just need to get moving and keep my eyes on my own stuff, instead of spending so much time obsessing over what people will think of my profile."

"What might be the first small step to take?" I asked.

"It's digging up a photo to use for my profile picture," Suzanna replied.

"And when will you have that done by?" I probed, trying to help Suzanna pick up momentum.

"I can do it by the end of the week."

Over the course of the next few weeks, Suzanna got moving. She took the small steps toward developing her LinkedIn profile that we discussed, and felt supported during our regular check-ins.

While Suzanna's fears were specifically about this particular social media platform, I see the presence of fear all the time in my work with clients who are considering a career change.

We feel fear whenever we venture into territory that is outside of our comfort zone, or when we feel unsafe on some level. Our fear has a job, and that job is evolutionary: to warn us of danger so that we can protect ourselves from harm. We are all wired to survive, and fear is part of that wiring.

Let's take the simple example of what it feels like to take a walk from point A to point B. You wouldn't feel fear as you walk from your kitchen to your bedroom because it is a totally familiar experience. However, you might feel fear if you were walking in an unfamiliar part of town.

Fear is a natural emotion that comes up when we are considering the prospect of unfamiliar territory in any area of our lives, including moving towards a new career path. We aren't truly in danger in these situations, but our fear kicks in because the outcome of the situation is unknown. Our brain wants answers and stability, and when we make life changes, we deny our brain those desires. The result? Fear.

In these situations, the goal is to keep moving despite the discomfort and to make the desired change, even in the presence of fear. Sure, it will be tempting to try to ignore the fear or wait for it to go away, but ultimately, neither of these strategies is effective. The one and only way to make the fear eventually go away is to work through the experience you are afraid of, and to take away the sense of unfamiliarity. This is a practice, and it gets easier each time.

When making a career transition we want to work with our fears in the following manner.

1) Listen to the message your fear is trying to tell you. Remember: your fear will let you know which part of you feels unsafe. We want to treat our fear like a small

child or a frightened animal, asking it gently to come closer and tell us what's going on. We want to listen and express compassion for the fear.

2) Create a pocket of safety around the scary experience.

3) Take tiny actions in spite of feeling fear. This is critical!

4) Connect to your *why*. Get curious and ask yourself questions to get in touch with your deeper motivations. Why is it important to you to make this change? By holding this perspective, you can shift your focus away from your fears, and toward your values. This viewpoint will empower you to you rise above your fears.

CORE CONCEPTS

FREEZING AND BECOMING SUPER BUSY

The following concepts and exercises are based on the work of Bev Barnes. There are two common reactions to the sensation of fear that come up for people that are not helpful.

The first reaction is to freeze. A person feels fear but tries to make the feeling go away by staying away from the action, thought, or feeling that catalyzed the fear. All forward progress stops.

The second reaction is to fill one's time with anything *other than* the fear-inducing thing—to get super busy. The motivation here is to try to distract from the feeling of fear. Someone might pick up a large amount of volunteer projects or take up a very time consuming hobby or throw themselves into a new venture at work, all in an effort to keep themselves from experiencing the discomfort of fear.

In both cases, the remedy is to be present with your fear and recognize that it's supposed to be there! Listen to the messages that your fear is trying to tell you, and then get moving. You'll need to draw on your courage and move into discomfort to make progress.

POCKETS OF SAFETY

It's easier to do something frightening in one area of our lives when we feel that we are consciously supporting ourselves with sources of comfort and strength in other parts of our lives. Examples of pockets of safety may include leaning on a supportive friend for advice, sticking to an exercise routine that makes you feel energized, snuggling up with a blanket and a favorite movie, or digging into a favorite hobby. A pocket of safety is something that provides you with a sense of familiarity and security, and brings you feelings of peace and well-being. Connecting to these resources before or after tackling a challenging task can make the scary to-do item far less intimidating. It can also help you to feel more grounded in the midst of expanding your comfort zone.

FEAR SUCCESS PROCESS

We've all done scary things in our lives before—whether it's going away to college, moving to a new city, or asking someone out. You've undoubtedly felt nervousness or trepidation around going through a new experience at some point in your life. Since you're reading this, you've survived and made it to the other side. When you look back at how you successfully handled these once-intimidating events, you can use your personal experience as research. Reflect on past experiences to pick up clues on what might be helpful to you today as you contemplate shifting your career.

LOOKOUT!

It's tempting to cope with fear by waiting for it to go away or by distracting ourselves from what we're feeling. Resist the temptation, and choose to be willing to experience fear. Take small steps. The fear will not go away until you feel it and move through it. Remember you can sign up for my free resource, the Step-By-Step Career Change E-Course, at www.cardycareercoaching.com/bookgift to get weekly help with what steps are appropriate to take. My voice will also be there cheering you on as you work towards your goals.

Remember: making a change, big or small, doesn't need to start with huge, uncalculated risks. But you do want to try the small, scary thing in front of you. Get in the habit of pushing into and through your fears. In most cases your life or livelihood is not actually in danger. You'll feel so proud of yourself once you do the thing that scares you. Give it a go.

EXERCISES

TAKE ACTION

Pick one thing on the horizon that brings up fear for you. Ideally, try to pick something career related. If that is too intimidating, you can pick another productive to-do that is scaring you in another part of your life. The goal here is to build your experience and confidence around moving through fear. When you practice this, and even allow it to become a habit, the fear dissolves more quickly and with greater ease each time.

Write down the action here:

_____

_____

_____

_____

_____

_____

Write down when you will take this action:

_____

Prioritize taking this action. Make a plan for how you will incorporate this goal into your life.

_____

_____

_____

_____

_____

Follow through, move through the fear, and do it!

Utilize the following exercises to further support you with taking action you identified above.

LISTENING TO FEAR

1) Pick a test experience that feels frightening to you. Or choose something else in your life that brings up a lot of fear, something that you haven't been able to do because you've felt afraid. Write it in the space below.

_____

_____

_____

2) Close your eyes and imagine that you are about to take this particular action. Note your physical sensation of fear below.

_____

_____

_____

_____

3) Now name your physical sensation with a metaphor. Is it a fizzy water feeling? A knot in your stomach? Note the identifying image below.

_____

_____

_____

_____

4) Now ask this image what it needs at the moment. Does it have anything else to say to you? Note any messages from your fear below. Mentally thank your fear for communicating with you before moving on.

_____

_____

_____

_____

5) How can you apply your fear's message to the situation at hand?

_____

_____

_____

_____

_____

POCKETS OF SAFETY

Look at your fear's messages from the prior exercise.

Brainstorm ways that you could create pockets of safety to help you work through these fears. For example, you might visit a friend in a new area before moving there or learn more about a particular field before applying for a new job.

_____

_____

_____

_____

Now consider very small actions you could take in service of your goals. Choose action steps that seem almost *too* easy. If you think of a big step, take the time to break it down into its smaller components.

_____

_____

_____

_____

_____

LEARN YOUR FEAR SUCCESS PROCESS

Think of a time in your life when you were faced with a scary or difficult situation, and reflect on how you worked through it.

First, note the situation here.

_____

_____

Now consider what helped you cope with this circumstance. How were you able to deal with the fears that you felt? What supported you in making it through?

_____

_____

_____

_____

How could you apply this same process to your current career transition situation?

_____

_____

_____

_____

_____

COACH'S NOTE

Things that bring up fear are not all that unique. We're all afraid of failure, rejection, making mistakes, being vulnerable, being seen, and being judged. Put even more generally, we're all afraid of feeling pain and discomfort.

If we never allow ourselves to feel pain or discomfort, we avoid the sharp sting of disappointment—but we also keep ourselves from productive opportunities. When we live in this state of avoidance, we choose to live cramped, constrained versions of our own life—and there is actually tremendous pain in that experience. Our lives shrink when fear is our master.

Tapping into courage and pushing through fear inarguably leads to a more fulfilling life. In fact, the quality of your life increases in direct proportion to your willingness to experience productive discomfort.

Of course, there's a difference between feeling productive discomfort and making careless decisions that harm us. Productive discomfort is the result of choosing to endure fear-inducing experiences en route to your goals. For example, putting a barbell loaded up with heavy weights onto your back, squatting down, and trying to stand back up is painful. But it is ultimately productive, serving a goal of getting stronger.

In the same way, we need to build our muscle when it comes to working through fear in our lives. We need to practice this skill, and show ourselves that we can build strength, resilience, and patience. By doing so, we learn many things—including the fact that fear is temporary. It can be acutely uncomfortable, but it passes. Plus, great things often wait for us on the other side of our fears.

One time, I was out giving a talk on salary negotiation. An audience member had a question about asking for a raise. She noted that she felt a lot of trepidation around the topic. During the presentation we'd talked about strategies and mindsets around asking for a raise, so my response was that, yes, it was going to be scary.

"You have to grab your courage. You have to be willing to experience a potential 'no'. You have to know that there may be a bit of awkwardness around asking. Your palms may be sweating in the moment. But to get the raise you're looking for you have to ask. You have to go through that discomfort to get what you want."

Do the scary thing in front of you. Do that scary thing enough, and you'll soon learn that there really isn't anything to be afraid of. You're human, so you're going to make mistakes. The people around you are also human, so they're going to judge you at times. But you're strong enough to handle both of these possibilities with grace and good humor. Better still, you'll give yourself the opportunity to learn, to improve, to grow stronger, and to live a large and fulfilling life.

CAREER MYTH: YOU NEED TO SEE EVERYTHING BEFORE YOU CAN GET STARTED

One of my wonderful clients shared a story with me that I often reference, because it's so relevant to the process of navigating a career change.

The story goes something like this. When my client was a kid, he went to visit his grandmother. During their visit, his grandmother took him to the front door of the house, turned off all the lights, handed him a flashlight, and told him to walk through the house to the back door without bumping into anything.

He carefully made his way through the house, shining the flashlight in front of him to avoid running into anything. Once he made it to the back of the house, his grandmother asked him, "How did you do that? How did you get all the way from the front of the house to the back when you couldn't see the back door when you started?"

The answer, of course, was that he could clearly see what was right in front of him, so he could take those initial steps. Each time he moved forward a bit more, he could see farther.

This experience holds true for careers too, and it presents a helpful metaphor for thinking about the incremental nature of big change. You probably will not be able to see the totality of where your career exploration or your next career step will wind up taking you for the next 20 years. But you can see what seems like a good decision for you at this juncture of your life. By taking that step you will be able to see farther and make your next decision about your career.

You don't have to have your career all figured before you get moving. Getting moving is what will help you figure it out.

Another element that goes hand in hand with fear is confidence. In the next chapter, I'll address frameworks for understanding confidence and strategies for building it. After all, everything is easier when you're feeling secure in yourself and your capabilities.

Chapter 10

RAISING YOUR CONFIDENCE

---

*Our career paths and work environments have
a huge influence on our confidence. In turn, our
level of confidence affects our ability to maneuver
our career in a new direction. If you're having
issues with confidence as you contemplate making
changes, don't fret. Luckily, confidence can
be improved.*

Delila, a 35-year-old woman living in a Maryland suburb of DC, was married to a kind and generous man who happened to also be the owner of a successful architecture firm. The pair had two young children, and Delila had worked part-time in the marketing department at her husband's firm for the past six years. This set-up was meant to give her the benefit of engaging her own professional development, while also providing her with the flexibility to be home with the kids. Sounds ideal, right?

The set-up was well intentioned, but the execution of this arrangement left a lot to be desired. Delila reached out to me because she felt unhappy in her current role and lost as to what to do next. When I dug deeper to understand her situation, several alarm bells went off.

Delila had been given a leadership role within the marketing department of her husband's architecture firm without having any prior work experience in marketing. While her title and take home pay were impressive, her actual engagement with her work was minimal, due to her lack of experience in the work. The rest of the marketing team excluded her from their work and decisions. Delila truly wanted to feel more engaged with the work, but simply didn't have the knowledgebase required to insert herself more forcefully into the team.

As a result, Delila's time in the office was spent doing a bit of entry-level work and a lot of watching the clock. She was bored and unchallenged by her day-to-day experience, and didn't know what to do about it. When Delila's husband would introduce her as his VP of Marketing at firm functions, she felt like a complete fraud, and she worried that she wouldn't have been able to find a job at all if it hadn't been for her husband giving one to her.

To make matters worse, Delila had recently overheard a conversation between two of the firm's senior leadership that had cast her capabilities in a negative light. Delila was extremely hurt and affected by these comments, but kept them to herself. Instead of talking to someone about her feelings, she internalized the judgments of her coworkers, and began to see herself through a lens of negativity. She felt insecure, inadequate, and embarrassed by her professional identity.

This convergence of events—an unearned title, an understimulating daily routine, and negative feedback from people she respected—caused Delila's confidence to plummet. She noticed herself being increasingly curt with her husband and in a near-constant funk.

As I got to know Delila more, it became apparent that she would be an excellent candidate for my Phoenix Rising coaching program. In spite of her current feelings about herself, Delila was actually an accomplished, sharply intelligent woman with an incredible fighting spirit. She had graduated with honors from an Ivy League college, where she'd been captain of the swim team and very active in volunteering with Habitat for Humanity. We'd need a more extended period of time working together to re-build her satisfaction with life and her confidence, but I knew from her past history that she was certainly capable of picking herself back up.

"There are a couple of things going on here," I reassured Delila, "but the biggest issue you're facing right now is a lack of confidence. You're a strong, intelligent, obviously capable person, but I can tell that you're not seeing that right now. And I totally get that. The boring day to day, the mismatched title, the negative comments you overheard—all of those factors have come together to make you feel less sure of yourself."

I wanted to emphasize to Delila that her current feelings about herself were not an accurate depiction of her actual capabilities. I explained to her that our work together would help clean up a portion of her muddied feelings. From there, we would work actively to re-build her self-confidence.

Delila seemed almost immediately relieved as she listened to me. "That sounds really good," Delila responded. "I know logically what you're saying is true, and my husband tells me all the time that I'm better than I think I am. It's just hard to feel that way right now."

"I know. We'll take it one step at a time and get you to a better place," I said.

Delila and I worked through several exercises together. We

questioned the negative beliefs she had internalized from the overheard conversation. We looked for evidence of her abilities by reflecting on her past experiences, and found myriad examples of how she had handled challenges successfully. Each of these steps helped Delila begin to shift her perspective. We worked through the compassion and forgiveness exercise for her and her husband's decisions over the prior six years. Delila experienced a dramatic lightbulb moment when she realized that her husband had never meant to put her in a difficult position. She reported an immediate improvement in their relationship once this clicked.

In the midst of this internal work, I emphasized that Delila would need to take on tasks that would both be challenging and doable. Since her current work environment was highly-charged for her, Delila decided to pursue a venture in the volunteer realm. She reconnected with Habitat for Humanity through her local chapter and offered to serve on their Board of Advisors. While she was initially tentative to share her ideas, her extensive experience with the organization in college quickly drew her out of her shell. She noticed that she felt more herself in this new environment than she had in a long time.

With this win under her belt, Delila saw an opportunity to build a partnership between her husband's architecture firm and the volunteer organization with which she was becoming more and more involved. She had the idea of possibly hosting a firm sponsored fundraising event for Habitat for Humanity, which she ran by her husband and then talked over with a supportive member of the firm's marketing team. With their green light, Delila took the lead on putting together the event and accompanying promotional materials.

"I actually look forward to going to work now," Delila told

me with a palpable increase in confidence. "There's so much to do, and the team has been surprisingly helpful. I'm learning a ton."

Over the course of many weeks, Delila and I continued to employ the dual strategies of cleaning up her mindset and actively pursuing "right sized" challenges that would help her to increase her sense of self efficacy. She's much more engaged with her work, her relationship with her husband has improved, and her feeling of self-worth is steadily growing. She and her husband also decided to change her title to more accurately reflect her actual marketing skillset, which she says is a huge relief.

CORE CONCEPT

PROPERTIES OF CONFIDENCE

In life, we're either building our confidence or depleting it. Confidence is both perishable and renewable. We may have felt confident in ourselves in the past, but this feeling can become depleted in environments that are negative or unchallenging. That said, confidence can be renewed by immersing ourselves in supportive and healthy environments that provide us with productive challenges through which we can be successful.

LOOKOUT!

GIVE YOURSELF THE OPPORTUNITY TO SUCCEED

Be careful of picking a goal that is far beyond your current confidence, experience, or ability level. It can be fun and exciting to dream about taking actions that seem larger than life. But if they are actually so large that you can't get a foothold with them, they aren't serving you. I prefer for my clients to initially break off a smaller chunk to work on. We're looking for something that is engaging and a bit of a stretch, but that also offers you a good opportunity for success.

An added benefit of taking a smaller chunk is that it provides you with the chance to adjust your course. One of my clients had decided that returning to graduate school was her next step, but she still harbored doubts about the decision. The idea that helped her move forward was to sign up for one semester of courses before formally entering the Master's program she had her eye on. This allowed her to feel out her decision experientially, while still providing her the comfort that she was not yet committed to a full two year program. In this case, she did, in fact, decide to continue on, but having that smaller goal to begin with was precisely what gave her the confidence to make the larger decision.

EXERCISES

CONFIDENCE BOOST

Make a list of difficult experiences you've endured, compliments you've received, and any other noteworthy moments in which you felt some sense of victory, and which invite you to feel a sense of confidence. These can span the personal and professional realms. They can also be current or from a while ago. They can be big or small items. Challenge yourself to come up with more examples than you think you can.

BUILD YOUR CONFIDENCE

1) Pick a goal to attempt. This goal can relate to any area

of life, but make sure to pick something that interests you. We're ideally looking for something that challenges you, but is also in the realm of feasibility. I recommend something that can be completed in one to three months.

Write your goal here:

_____

_____

_____

_____

2) Check yourself.

- Does your goal feel light or heavy? Does it feel like a healthy challenge, or an insurmountable punishment?
- Are you fighting your nature or honoring it? For example, you are fighting your nature if you know you work better on a team, but you have given yourself a goal that has you working in isolation.
- Would you need to be super human to achieve this? Or would it be possible given all the other demands on your time?
- Is your goal too easy? Or is it right at the edge of your comfort zone?
- Is your goal specific and measurable? Will you know when you've achieved it?

_____

_____

_____

_____

_____

3) Rework your goal until you hit on something that is clear, specific, energizing, supportive, and just the right amount of challenge. Write your finalized goal here.

_____

_____

_____

_____

_____

4) Make a plan to achieve your goal.

_____

_____

_____

_____

_____

5) Stick with it until you get it.

6) Note your overall confidence level has increased.

7) Repeat.

COACH'S NOTE

The first time I spoke in front of my Toastmasters club (an organization that helps people practice public speaking), I was so nervous that my voice trembled audibly and my hands shook visibly. I really wanted to do a good job. Yet I was a novice speaker, and even the friendly crowd of people at Toastmasters felt intimidating to me. I wished I had more confidence, but I stood up and participated with my shaky presentation skills anyway. I knew that the only way to get better at speaking was to go through the initial awkward stages.

I kept at it. Speaking was something that I wanted to do well, so I kept trying. I pushed myself to speak at venues outside of my Toastmasters club, even to crowds of hundreds of people. Some of the speeches I gave when I was learning were better than others, but over time, I improved significantly.

Now people compliment my speaking all the time and often ask me how I'm able to speak so naturally and with such confidence. The answer is incredibly simple: I just worked on it, again and again.

Push yourself. Extend your comfort zone. Try something that challenges you. And, this one is important: don't give up until you accomplish what you set out to do. You will start out feeling uneasy, but by the time you finish, your confidence will soar.

If you could use a supportive voice in your ear (and by ear, I mean inbox), sign up for my complimentary Step-By-Step Career Change E-Course at www.cardycareercoaching. com/bookgift. I'll kindly remind you of your worth and challenge you to build your own confidence over the course of several weeks.

CAREER MYTH: BEING FREE OF OBLIGATIONS IS WHERE IT'S AT

Do you ever dream of living your life fully at ease? Sitting on the beach? Retiring and being able to just relax and enjoy life?

I had an experience in college that stripped me of the illusion that living in a perma-vacation would be a good thing.

So much of my time in high school was spent ignoring my own well-being in service of doing school work, playing sports, and being around friends. When I reached college, I swung way over to the other side of the spectrum, deciding for once I would just focus on myself and what I wanted.

I attended my classes and participated in a few extracur-riculars—but honestly, my main goal in life at the time was to reach some pinnacle of physical health and well-being. I aspired to feel good, the way a well-fed, tuckered out toddler feels good as they're being snuggled into cozy bedding.

There was only one problem. I didn't really feel that good, despite this being my ostensible goal.

In fact, I felt lonely. Unfulfilled. Lost. Bored.

What I didn't understand at the time, and what took me a few years to figure out, was that I needed to connect to a purpose for my life beyond my own well-being. We are healthiest when we are connected to others, supporting them in their goals, and receiving support for our own.

After my college graduation, I let go of my mythical dream of total health and well-being in favor of spending time culti-vating relationships that mattered to me and work that would be meaningful. There were nights when I slept enough and nights when I didn't. Days when I ate well and days when I didn't. Yet, on the whole, I felt so much better than I ever felt in college. I was thriving by adding back in the obligations that I had initially set out to strip away.

Today my metrics for well-being encompass a much broader range of questions than the set I used in college. Questions like:

Am I being a good partner, friend, and family member?

Am I contributing to the world and being of service to others?

Am I challenging myself, pursuing dreams, and growing?

It's important to take care of ourselves and to do our best to be healthy. But the reason why is *not* because doing so is a destination. It's important because feeling well and having plenty of emotional and physical energy enables us do a better job at whatever is in front of us, especially if we are aiming to make some kind of positive contribution to the world in our personal or professional lives.

Sitting on a beach for the rest of our lives may sound appealing when we're on the brink of burnout from our work. We may think a boring or easy job would be a step up if we are constantly stressed out at our jobs. But we actually want stress and challenge—at an appropriate level. Without having some element of resistance to overcome in our professional, intellectual, and creative lives, our confidence erodes, and our sense of well-being diminishes.

This chapter and the prior seven chapters focused on the most common reasons people get stuck at a career crossroads. The next chapter shifts to a topic that floats around in many people's minds when it comes to considering possible career changes: Entrepreneurship, being your own boss, and starting a business.

Chapter 11

CONSIDERING ENTREPRENEURSHIP

---

*The majority of my clients maneuver from a job
in one career to a job in another career, but
the idea of starting a business has also popped
across many of their radar screens. This is not a
book about starting a business, but doing so is
one career option that folks consider, so I thought
it relevant to include. In this chapter, I share my
personal career story, since starting a business is a
route that I've been down.*

I feel a lot of compassion for my clients who are at a career
crossroads because for several years early in my career I felt
exactly the same way, and I dealt with many of the same issues.

My main career desire early in my career was Fulfillment.
Personal Well-Being was a close second. I wholeheartedly
believed that the most important thing I could do would be to
find a career I was passionate about.

So it was extremely disheartening and frustrating when I
found myself on a career path that wasn't personally engaging.
I worked as a government contractor doing audit work, which
meant I saw a lot of basements while sampling financials to

verify their accuracy. The job was decent and paid well, and I think that with a more mature perspective I could have had a better experience in the world of accounting, though it probably wouldn't have ever been my forte.

At the time I was unhappy with my day-to-day at work. I was bored. When I stopped to think about it, I dreaded the idea that this was to be my life.

I struggled with my social environment, too much intro-spection, and a lack of confidence. My wonderful parents had generously helped me to get set up with a financially-reward-ing career path, so there was a strong social pressure to stay in that field. Like my clients, I thought about my career direction a lot. A few years ago, I cleared out an old drawer and found a thick stack of printouts and scribbled notes about graduate school and job opportunities (none of which I ever acted on). I kept trying to think my way to an answer. And, finally, it had been a number of years since I'd been challenged by my day to day, which meant my confidence was at a low point.

After floundering for quite some time, I decided to take a smaller set of actions that flowed from my personal inter-ests. I began three ventures to try to get traction. I joined a writer's group. I mentored students after school. And I vol-unteered with a crisis and suicide hotline. The hotline made the biggest impression on me. After feeling like a duck out of water in business school, I was relieved and excited to interact with the other volunteers—they felt like kindred spirits. While the work was nerve-wracking at times, I received phe-nomenal training, and found the work itself rewarding. I was also good at it and was eventually selected to be a trainer of other volunteers.

With this experience under my belt, I began to feel enthusi-astic about the possibility of pursuing counseling-type work.

But every time I looked into graduate schools, I fixated on the timeline—there would be many years of schooling to endure before I could actually do what I wanted—help people. I was impatient and wanted to get started cultivating my new life right away.

It was in this state of mind that I saw a promotion for a life coach training with an author whose work I really respected. I signed up, thinking at the time that becoming a life coach would be a short cut to getting to do helping work.

As I got into the training I started thinking about leaving my auditing job to work on coaching full time. I went back and forth on the decision. It was scary to consider. Going into business for myself was a huge unknown. I remember being out on a bike ride and feeling a strong physical reaction of fear as I made the mental decision that I was going to leave.

Without thinking much beyond my desire to do fulfilling work and my innate pull towards being helpful, I fell onto the path of entrepreneurship.

Looking back, I see I made this decision with the utmost naiveté possible. I didn't talk to people working in helping professions to scope out the landscape because I was so worried that someone would try to talk me out of my decision. I'd made a practice of doing things that scared me (in a healthy way) with good results in the past, and this felt like an extension of that habit, so I ignored my loved one's concerns. I mistook my huge desire to get out of my day-to-day drudgery and my enthusiasm for coaching work for an indicator of my capability at running a business.

One freshly pressed website and two months later, reality came to call. I didn't know what I was doing. I didn't know how to find clients. I wasn't making any money in my new venture.

I knew I didn't want to go back to accounting. I knew I preferred "people stuff". I didn't have much confidence in my professional abilities, and I didn't want to take a job that would be compelling enough to pull me away from my chosen path (or that would creep into the evening hours I was planning on working on my business).

So I took a job as a nanny for a lovely family. Working as a nanny is not rocket science, but it was more challenging than the data entry-level work I'd been doing at my prior job. Through this job, my confidence slowly grew. It was hard at times, and I had good days and bad days, but overall I was good at it. I found I had a lot of patience. I learned I was good at being consistent and setting up routines. I connected with a goofy, creative side I didn't realize I had.

During the early years of my business, I gradually decreased my time working as a nanny and increased my time working on my business. The steady income helped support me through the learning curve of my entrepreneurial venture. I worked with four families over the course of four years and regularly babysat for at least eight more, which gave me a lot of insight into how careers and families intersect.

During this period I kept working on figuring out how to grow a business. The first time through anything takes longest, and the first time through when I only had a handful of hours a week took me even longer. Gradually, I learned and made progress. Mostly, I learned that it's never one thing that makes a business go; it's a series of consistent efforts.

I'm a stubborn optimist, so I kept at it, always thinking I'd have it down with my next effort. I initially believed a lot of hype about what was possible as a small business owner. I faced many disappointments. I pushed through fear after fear and let myself and my work be more and more visible. It was often a struggle to get through my day job when what I really wanted to be doing was something else.

I eventually transitioned to running my business full-time. My skill at helping my clients improved as the number of clients I'd worked with increased and my experience grew. I've learned what works for people and made mistakes that helped me learn about what didn't.

I got into entrepreneurship to be helpful to people, and I've found my work with clients to be tremendously rewarding. It's wonderful to know the right thing to do to move a person forward. There are literally times I jump up and down after working with a client, because I'm so excited that I've been of service. One of the things I love to do most is talk with people about what matters most to them, and I get to regularly have those conversations in my profession.

A big downside to my business was that in the early stages cash flow was unpredictable month-to-month. I never knew what I would be earning. I went through slow months when I worried about how I'd pull through. I'm not normally a big spender, but I became even more frugal.

I was able to make it through this phase because I didn't have a family of my own, I worked a day job during the early years, and my husband gave me a financial boost when I went full-time to coaching. My business also happens to have extremely low overhead, so I was able to keep trying without ever incurring debt. Many business owners do not have these same luxuries.

There are consequences to my decisions too. I wasn't saving for retirement during the lean years of working to get my business off the ground, and that's something I will need to be particularly mindful of moving forward. Over time, my values have shifted from a strong Fulfillment focus (without much regard to financial goals) to incorporating a Financial focus onto my radar screen as well.

On the business side of things, my biggest learning curve has been the marketing element. I spend a lot of time on activities geared toward letting people know that I exist and that I can help them with career concerns. That means that part of my work involves doing "job search"-type activities almost every day—something I certainly didn't expect when I initially started my path as a life coach. I am constantly putting myself out there for rejection. (You have no idea how much rejection I regularly endure. Now it slides off my back. It's simply part of the job.) Luckily, I find the marketing component to be a puzzle. It is stimulating and interesting, and I like doing it.

This promotional work has helped me hone my project management skills; I've taken on bigger and bigger marketing projects. I've learned about hiring and managing help. I've grown as a speaker and have given over a hundred speeches. I eventually figured out that I'm good at following through and executing projects I set out to accomplish.

As a business grows it becomes a lot more about creating systems and managing teams. I do have the freedom and autonomy to choose the business' direction and the content of my days, but I am also still beholden to the market and my clients' needs.

It's been a very long road so far. The short-cut I so eagerly jumped at turned out to be full of traffic, potholes, and detours. Building a business from scratch is a lot of work. Folks who start it with more confidence, connections, or cash can go much faster than I did, but it's always a serious undertaking. Getting a new business off the ground is the equivalent of moving a mountain. You can't do it in one go, and it takes a huge effort and an incredible degree of patience.

Pushing myself to do the scary thing and sticking with it helped me to identify and build my strengths, learn what works in my business, and boost my confidence in the process. What I'm able to accomplish today, nearly seven years from the day I opened my doors, is incredibly different than when I began. The combination of knowledge, experience, and self-assurance I now possess is night and day from those early days.

I don't regret my choices—they've made me who I am and taught me a ton, though it has not been easy. And I would never discourage anyone who wanted to take this path from doing so. Moving a mountain is inarguably a lot of work, but who you become after doing that work is someone with a lot more strength, bravery, focus, and self-trust. My plan is to stick with my business, but I now see that joining an awesome team of an existing business could also be a wonderful option. (In fact, I've had business owner clients who have decided to make this switch.)

I hope reading my story and the following information helps you to have a fuller understanding of what entrepreneurship really entails, because I think there are a lot of dreams and hopes that are tied up in entrepreneurship that don't mesh with the reality.

CORE CONCEPT

THE SMALL BUSINESS STORY IS PREDICTABLE

If you're thinking of starting a small business, I recommend *The E-Myth*, by Michael Gerber. Gerber notes that many small businesses are started by so-called "technicians," people who excel at a particular skill. Two other terms Gerber uses in his schema are the "entrepreneur" role (the visionary) and the "manager" role (the one who makes sure everything gets done). He also describes the process of growth for small businesses, noting that there are predictable levels of success along the way, and that each level requires a different mindset. In one section, Gerber explains that those who feel called to do more technical work (e.g. work without the other elements of running a business) will prefer the role of employee. I agree with this assessment.

Consider the following pros and cons of working as an employee and as an entrepreneur. Which elements are important to you? Which elements are "deal-breakers"?

Type of Work	Pros	Cons
Employee	Steady Paycheck	Not in Complete Control
	Natural Community	Income Cap
Entrepreneur	Lots of Control	Responsible for the Risk
	Freedom to Set Schedule	Isolating
	Potential for Higher Financial Reward	Heavy Workload

LOOKOUT!

There are those who are in the business of selling people the dream of entrepreneurship. In many instances, these are businesses that target people who are interested in changing careers, particularly people who want to pump up the passion-element in their careers. These businesses present entrepreneurship as the answer, and hype the attractive elements of business ownership, such as flexibility, freedom, and doing work you love. Many times, these businesses tout their personal success as entrepreneurs as evidence that you, too, will be successful. They sell programs or coaching that will show you their path to success.

If you decide business ownership is the path for you, it can be helpful to learn from and participate in business building programs like those that I've described above. There's definitely a place for them, and there are people leading these offerings who are well intentioned and genuine in their desire to help.

But recognize that selling the dream of entrepreneurial success is a business, and one that's different from most other businesses. There's often more financial reward in selling dreams than in pursuing dreams. Who do you think makes more consistent money in most cases—the person selling yoga teacher training or the person teaching classes?, the person selling drums or the drummer? It's usually the person selling the dream. Pursuing your dream could be a great next step, and I believe dreams are worthwhile. But be aware of the economic realities of your choices as you're making these big decisions.

EXERCISES

In the same vein as the test experiences exercise in Chapter 8, consider how you could test out entrepreneurship. You could try a side project, take a vocation vacation, attend a meeting of a group of entrepreneurs (there are lots of these!), or do work for a small business to expose yourself to the back-end of what it takes.

Brainstorm ideas for how you could you test entrepreneurship, if it's something you're interested in.

_____

_____

_____

_____

_____

COACH'S NOTE

My client, Zach, earned a great salary at a job that he hated. Through the course of our work we determined that the path that he'd always most wanted to go down was that of owning his own business. He'd loved the process of remodeling his own home, but had been frustrated by the lack of quality contractors in his area. His dream was to open a company that specialized in quality renovations.

Zach was the main breadwinner in his family and had two kids, so jumping ship and diving head first into his new venture felt overwhelmingly scary. He worried about whether he could succeed and turn a profit fast enough. When we spoke, I agreed with Zach's assessment that hasty decision-making would be unwise. Making an immediate 180 degree career change would set him up for failure and threaten his family's well-being. Zach and I talked about the learning curve he'd need to experience, the skills he'd need to develop, and the network he'd have to build in order to be successful. We built a plan together about the milestones toward which he could work while still keeping his current job for income's sake.

This approach fit with Zach's risk tolerance and his priorities. In other cases, a more aggressive plan could be in order. Choose the option that honors your responsibilities and sets you up for the highest chance of success.

CAREER MYTH: THE ONLY WAY TO DO WHAT YOU LOVE IS TO WORK FOR YOURSELF

There are plenty of ill-fitting jobs and bad work environments out there. If you find yourself in one of these situations, it's a quick leap to think that the only way to have a good day at work is to strike out on your own and create a great work environment for yourself. This is an option, but it's not the only option—and often, starting your own business is more challenging than rewarding at the get-go.

Recognize that when you work for yourself you are actually trading in one boss for the "boss" of many customers. There will always be constraints on what you can do, and you'll need to line up with the market demand. Work still needs to get done, and establishing the structure and discipline to execute that work rests squarely on your shoulders. You will have fewer resources on your own (at least initially) than you would with a company with more stability and man-power.

After a lot of upfront effort, being your own boss can

become a good gig, but the benefits are simply not going to be available to you on day one. Know that there are many options that could improve your work life. Just because you aren't seeing great jobs with healthy cultures from the vantage point of your particular office window does not mean that they don't exist. Many companies purposely aim to create excellent environments to attract top talent. Others encourage an entrepreneurial attitude within the context of the organization. Keep the full range of possibilities in mind, and evaluate whether or not you want to take on the risk and challenge of entrepreneurship.

We've now covered the bulk of the reasons why people get stuck at a career crossroads and looked at different career path possibilities. Let's wrap things up in the next chapter.

Chapter 12

CONTINUING YOUR JOURNEY

---

*Over the past few chapters, you've met a
sampling of my clients and have read about a
segment of our work together. You're probably
wondering what happened next. This chapter will
give you a sense of the outcome of their stories
and will hopefully provide you with momentum
and encouragement for your own journey.*

A my, the mediator from Chapter 1, turned out to have an
incredible knack for graphic design. Her major in college had
been Art History, but she'd left her visual interests behind
and earned a law degree to boost her job prospects. Through
our work together Amy pulled out her old passion, talked
to people in the field of graphic design, and began building
a small portfolio of freelance jobs. So far the work has been
rewarding, and Amy is almost to the point where she will be
ready to submit her portfolio to a design firm.

Sergey, the athletic medical school applicant from Chapter
2, made the decision to leave his medical school dream behind
once and for all. He researched going back to school to get

an engineering degree and began thinking through how he could gain relevant work experience (and income) while being a full-time student in this new field.

Rama, the hyper-organized woman from Chapter 3, is fresh off of a great year in her new job as a community manager and is in the process of applying for graduate school programs that will continue to further her career as a curriculum designer.

Maggie, the burnt-out chef from Chapter 4, slowly but surely recovered her strength and confidence in herself. She decided to re-tool her experience into her own small business as a personal chef for busy families. To support her well-being, she brought on two assistants to help her with the prep work and cooking. She still works hard, but her stress level has decreased tremendously, and she's being much more attentive to other areas of her life—like her health and relationships.

Mason, the actor from Chapter 5 who sought financial independence from his family, has gotten more and more engaged with his work as part of the sales team for the regional plumbing company where he is employed. He's been surprised at how much he enjoys the work and is incredibly proud of a recent promotion. He feels empowered from the financial success he's achieved thus far, and is using it as a jumping off point to continue extricating himself from his financial dependence on his family. Acting is still a part of his life—he performs at a community theatre in his area regularly—but it has become less significant.

Tom, the lawyer from Chapter 6, is working through his short-term goal of staying at his job for a year to boost his savings. He's joined a professional digital marketing organization and regularly attends their events. Sometimes he still feels frustrated and impatient to move on, but he's sticking with his plan, and is excited to be moving toward an exit from his career as a lawyer.

Jaime, the IT superstar with an interest in helping professions from Chapter 7, is continuing to develop his mentoring and people skills in his management role at work. He started a meetup group on personal development topics to further explore his interests.

Claire, the researcher from Chapter 8, networked her way into the Environmental Programs Analyst job that she had identified during our time working together. She picked a target company that she wanted to work for and doggedly reached out to every member of the organization over the course of several months. (And yes, she certainly felt frustrated at times during those long weeks of planting seeds.) She got the job.

Suzanna, the woman who felt terrified of putting up her LinkedIn profile from Chapter 9, took small steps and experienced several periods of stalling out, but she eventually got her profile done. She's slowly reconnecting with former colleagues and is in the process of applying for a new job.

Delila, the woman who worked in marketing for her husband's architecture firm in Chapter 10, continued to build her confidence as she tapped into her particular strengths and skills in the work environment. She became increasingly integrated into the firm as she learned how to apply her interests to her work, and now actively engages in the firm's culture as a confident member of the team.

You read about my story in Chapter 11. I'm still learning and growing as a business owner and am constantly working to deliver great service to my clients. As of this writing I run Cardy Career Coaching (www.cardycareercoaching.com)

and a women's group in the DC area, Belleconnecta (www.belleconnecta.com). With both ventures, I aspire to help people improve their lives.

The aforementioned stories are demonstrative of the core concepts I work with, but I would be remiss to ignore the multitude of other clients with whom I've worked. I've had the pleasure of working with so many wonderful individuals who often present unique cases beyond the general principles I've outlined.

Here's a brief overview of select other scenarios.

Some clients have stayed in the same industry, but switched to a better environment. Others have begun volunteer work related to the field they're interested in and are building up experience and confidence to aid them in making a more formal switch. Several have incorporated a move to a new area into a career change and are re-building their lives in fresh surroundings. A handful are going full throttle at challenging dreams. A few have decided to leave family businesses and legacies to forge their own paths.

There are also the folks who are still working through things in their own way and in their own time. For instance, some have conducted a job search for a job that isn't what they really want. Others have gone back to a familiar type of work that they'd previously had issues with, rather than trying something new. A couple of clients have left our work in a drawer and are holding out for something easier to come their way. Life happens to people too. Babies are born. Spouses move. Loved ones become ill. Things just get busy. And as a result, personal career dreams get put on the back burner. Not every client's story resolves itself in the context of our work together. I think we all need to learn our own lessons, and sometimes that takes time.

With all the stories I've told, you'll also notice that there isn't a definitive ending. My clients' lives and careers are still in progress. They will continue to refine and revise their career paths based on their Career Strategies, which will change over time.

In the end, I can deliver on clarity and helping clients to make a plan, but it is their business whether they follow through with taking action or not. In the best cases, I'm able to see clients all the way through their transition. In other cases I know I've been able to help them move forward, even if they aren't all the way at their goals. In all cases, I know that I've given my clients the opportunity to connect to their desires, to be heard, and encouragement to step more fully into the lives they want to be leading.

CORE CONCEPTS

MY TOP 12 CAREER LESSONS

1) We're all looking for our own unique mix of fulfillment, financial health, and personal well-being. There isn't one right answer, and what's right for you may differ from what's right for your loved ones.

2) We all come to things in our own time.

3) You know what you want better than anyone else around you. It's up to you to chart your course and set sail before other people can see the shore.

4) Challenging life events knock down even the strongest people. Enduring a tough time is not a personal failing. Make sure to forgive yourself for the times when you

weren't a superhero, and send compassion to yourself as you reflect upon whatever it was that you went through.

5) If you feel like you can't do something, take a step back and consider the way you're thinking about it. Try to find a more gentle and productive perspective.

6) Keep an eye on the career desires you may have been neglecting. Even if they aren't your top priority, it's good to keep them on your radar screen.

7) Set up coffee dates. Find someone you like and check in on one another. Create support systems and a vibrant network of people you enjoy. Attend events. Ask for help. Don't go it alone.

8) Real world experiences relating to career trump our imagination almost every time.

9) Embrace doing the hard stuff (e.g. experiencing rejection, making mistakes, feeling discomfort, not getting it right on the first try) to get the good stuff.

10) You are either building your confidence by regularly doing hard things or you are eroding it.

11) Aim for a mix of courage and compassion in everything you do. Go towards doing the hard, scary thing. Be kind to yourself when you make a mistake. Recognize that you're human. Everyone has bad days. Let 'em go and try again tomorrow.

12) Careers evolve over time. What you want today will be different from what you want in a decade. Adjust your career to what matters most to you.

LOOKOUT!

You've made it (nearly) to the end of this book—congratulations! You now know a lot more about the process of navigating a career crossroads and are better equipped to handle obstacles in your own situation.

Unfortunately, however, reading a book is not enough to transition your career to a better place. The critical next step is follow through and actually try to implement the exercises and frameworks presented in this book.

If you'd like further support on implementing the steps, please sign up for the Step-By-Step Career Change E-Course at www.cardycareercoaching.com/bookgift. I'll send you a bite sized step to take care of each week to help you stay on track. A book can be read in a week. A career change takes longer, which is why I've added this continuing support option for readers who are serious about making a change and could use additional accountability and support. And, really, who couldn't? Sign up at www.cardycareercoaching.com/bookgift. I'd be happy to continue our journey together.

EXERCISES

ACKNOWLEDGEMENT OF PROGRESS

When you're working to improve any aspect of your own personal life, including your career, there is no external boss or other authority figure to praise your progress or acknowledge your efforts. As a result, this task will fall on you.

In my experience, taking a few minutes every so often to reflect on what you've been working on and how things have been going is a powerful exercise. You might consider the lessons you've learned, the actions you've taken, or the accomplishments you've been able to complete.

When we're taking the time to acknowledge our progress, we want to look at ourselves with kindness. Focus on what has been achieved rather than what is still remaining. Celebrate the small wins. Offer yourself encouragement to continue on. Note the real strengths that you're bringing to the table, if only for the sake of this exercise.

What have you achieved so far as you've worked through this book? (Note that nearly completing the book counts!)

_____

_____

_____

_____

_____

_____

_____

_____

_____

_____

_____

_____

_____

CONNECTING TO YOUR VALUES

Taking steps toward creating a life that lines up with your core desires is bound to bring up a whole host of thoughts and feelings. Some will feel amazing. Some will not feel so great. Connecting to our values provides a compelling reason to endure the experience of our journey.

For example, I've shared that when I first began working on public speaking I felt nervous and uncomfortable in front of an audience. I allowed myself to feel these things and still took action because I hold the values of self-expression and personal development so strongly.

The negative feelings eventually passed as I grew more comfortable with speaking. My ability to get through that initial period was due in large part to my willingness to feel uncomfortable. By connecting to our values and prioritizing them, we become more equipped to handle tough emotions along our path, as we know how important it is for us to head in the direction of our ideals.

The following exercise is a modified version of an exercise from Russ Harris' book, *The Happiness Trap*.

My goal is to:

_____

_____

_____

_____

_____

This goal is important to me because . . . / The values that this goal rests on are . . . :

_____

_____

_____

_____

The things I'm willing to put up with in order to achieve this goal include:

_____

_____

_____

_____

As I'm working toward my goal, it would be helpful to keep the following ideas in mind:

_____

_____

_____

_____

WHEN ALL ELSE FAILS

As you are working through your career transition there are going to be times when you aren't sure how to keep going. When this happens, try one or more of the following strategies.

Ask for Help; Don't Go it Alone!

- Ask for help from a career coach or therapist.
- Ask for help from a supportive acquaintance, friend, or mentor.

Impact Your Physical Environment

- Go for a walk, or get moving in some way.
- Organize one small area of your life (a desk drawer, your purse or wallet, the center console in your car).

Take Constructive Action

- Clear one lingering item from your to-do list by getting it done.
- Find a super-small step forward relating to your career (draft the subject line of an email, print out directions to a club you want to join), and do it.

Expand Your Comfort Zone

- Go to a new event, talk to a new person, try a new activity; it doesn't have to be related to career at all, just practice getting outside of your comfort zone.
- Try something socially uncomfortable; this will vary depending on comfort level, but it could range from introducing yourself to a stranger to writing and publishing a blog post to going to a karaoke night.

Practice Compassion

- Be kind and encouraging to yourself.
- Cheer on progress, even small progress, as a great thing.

Connect with Gratitude

- List out several things in your life that you're grateful for.
- As you are connecting with your gratitude, pay attention to the physical feeling of gratefulness.

COACH'S NOTE

My sincere hope is that this book has helped you to have a better understanding of why you were having trouble figuring out your career direction. If you would like further support, please sign up for the Step-By-Step Career Change E-Course, a weekly guide that will help you make progress, at www.cardycareercoaching.com/bookgift, or consider working with me in one of my career coaching programs, which you can learn more about at www.cardycareercoaching.com/coaching. My team and I would be happy to help.

I've seen clients go through the process of making a career change many times. I have to be honest: people rarely go through this process in a perfectly straight line. More often than not, there's a fair bit of lurching around, of experimenting, shifting gears, and starting over.

But when people hang in there through the inevitable missteps and disappointments, they're ultimately successful. They walk into a new era of their careers and their identities. They become more connected to themselves and begin walking on a path they feel optimistic about and in alignment with. It takes work and a willingness to go through many uncomfortable feelings to get moving, but it is a huge relief to get un-stuck and onto a path forward.

Remember that you can make this change, too. Take things one step at a time. Be willing to put in the effort. Things rarely (if ever) go perfectly on the first try, so keep at it until you get what you want. Re-commit to the process when you get sidetracked. Do the things that scare you. And don't forget to be compassionate with yourself along the way. Get to work on creating a life that's completely your own.

Best wishes on your journey!

PS. I adore receiving updates, so if this book impacted you in any way, please, please, please let me know. The best way to get my attention is to leave a review on Amazon. I'd love to know what's changed for you as a result of reading *Career Grease*. Do you have a new perspective? An increased understanding of what to do next? Have you made progress on your career? Not only will you make my day by leaving a review, but you just might inspire someone else to improve their career with your story, which would be ah-mazing. Thanks in advance!

STEP-BY-STEP CAREER CHANGE E-COURSE

Keep your commitment to bettering your career top of mind by signing up for the Step-By-Step Career Change E-Course. Each week you'll receive instructions on a doable action step that will help you to make progress on improving your career, along with valuable reminders, words of encouragement, and a curated selection of quick-read blog posts that will support you and keep you on track.

Sign up for this free resource at www.cardycareercoaching.com/bookgift, and start improving your career today, one step at a time.

CAREER COACHING OFFERINGS

Alison Cardy has worked with hundreds of individuals to improve their careers. She offers three career coaching programs of varying intensity that are designed to help people increase their clarity, eliminate obstacles, and gain momentum on a positive career change. Her programs are designed to get results as fast as possible, while providing a safe and supportive coaching environment and superior customer service.

SIGNATURE PROGRAMS INCLUDE:

JUST GET ME POINTED IN THE RIGHT DIRECTION

Need a sounding board to talk through a potential career change? Interested in getting a personalized road map to follow to move your career forward? This short-term program provides you with devoted time, attention, and accountability to make progress on your career direction.

This program is best for folks who aren't sure which way to go, but know that once they connect to a career direction they'll be able to follow-through on moving towards it without much resistance.

CAREER DIRECTION CLARITY + ACTION PLAN

Would you like someone to walk you through the process of making a career change step-by-step? Do you sense that there are obstacles that you need to work through before you can make progress? This intensive program provides you with extended 1-1 attention and coaching to help you clear the path towards a brighter career future.

This program is intended to support people who feel very stuck in the process of making a career change. You've been trying to get results on your own, but aren't getting anywhere. You know you need more support to finally move forward.

PHOENIX RISING

Are you ready to make massive positive changes in your career and life? Have you been through a rough period and are now in the process of re-building? This long-term coaching program will aid you in stepping into a more confident and capable version of yourself. We'll work together to create the life you've been yearning to live.

This program is for strong, committed individuals who are interested in investing in improving their future. People who value personal growth and are willing to fully show up in the coaching process achieve amazing transformations in this program.

HOW TO GET STARTED WITH A CAREER COACHING PROGRAM

Go to www.cardycareercoaching.com/coaching, and follow the instructions on that page to begin the process of working in one of the above career coaching programs.

Note: These program descriptions are accurate at the time of publication. I regularly review my client data to determine how I can improve my services and adjust my programs accordingly.

KEYNOTE AND WORKSHOP OFFERINGS

Alison Cardy is an experienced speaker who has successfully delivered over 100 presentations to audiences ranging from 10 to 300 people.

SIGNATURE TALKS INCLUDE:

CAREER GREASE: HOW TO GET UNSTUCK AND PIVOT YOUR CAREER

Alison supports professionals with actively managing a career change in a fun, interactive environment. She assists attendees with looking at the big picture of where they want to be going with their career and provides them with navigational frameworks that will support them in making career decisions. Audience members go in depth as to why and where they are getting stuck in the career change process. They walk away with knowledge of the concrete steps they need to take to jumpstart progress, along with confidence to take ownership of their careers.

GROW YOUR PAYCHECK: PHRASES, STRATEGIES, AND MINDSETS YOU NEED TO KNOW TO GET WHAT YOU WANT

Alison helps attendees brush up on effective negotiation techniques for getting the compensation package they're most wanting, whether it is a specific dollar amount increase or another perk, like flex time, continuing education, or more vacation days. During this workshop Alison guides attendees through negotiation role plays in a comfortable and safe environment, teaches five core negotiation concepts, and pulls back the curtain on what may be causing them to feel uncomfortable or intimidated about asking for a more desirable employment package. Attendees will leave the presentation with an improved negotiation knowledge base, an increase in their negotiation confidence, and clarity on the blocks that have been holding them back.

BOOK ALISON FOR YOUR NEXT CAREER EVENT

Are you interested in having Alison speak at your next event or training? Excellent! Alison brings professionalism, experience, and a wonderful, supportive energy to every event she participates in. She consistently delivers both inspiration and actionable takeaways. Her speaking style involves storytelling, humor, and audience participation. She is based in Arlington, VA and is most readily available to speak to audiences in DC, Maryland, and Virginia (DC metro area).

Contact Alison via the contact form at www.cardycareercoaching.com/contact to schedule a speaking engagement. Please take the time to provide as many details as possible on your event in your email. Alison is regularly booked months in advance, so the more specific your answers, the faster we can get back to you!

ABOUT THE AUTHOR

Alison Cardy is a career coach who has guided hundreds of people to innovative and functional career solutions. She provides one-on-one coaching, group coaching, workshops, and keynote speeches. She is a practical advocate for achieving your heart's desires, improving your workweek, and making a difference, all while keeping an eye on your financial success. Alison and her work have been featured in the Washington Post, the Chicago Tribune, and the Huffington Post, as well as on Monster, Forbes, and LearnVest. She is a certified coach and a graduate of the University of Maryland's Smith School of Business. Her career coaching website is www.cardycareercoaching.com. She also runs a DC area women's group, Belleconnecta, which can be found at www.belleconnecta.com.

Made in the USA
Middletown, DE
14 April 2016